# Talk to Me

## Conversation Tips for the Small-Talk Challenged

CAROLE HONEYCHURCH, MA
ANGELA WATROUS

New Harbinger Publications, Inc.

*Publisher's Note*

*This publication is designed to provide accurate and authoritative information in regard to the subject matter covered. It is sold with the understanding that the publisher is not engaged in rendering psychological, financial, legal, or other professional services. If expert assistance or counseling is needed, the services of a competent professional should be sought.*

Distributed in Canada by Raincoast Books

Copyright © 2003 by Carole Honeychurch and Angela Watrous
New Harbinger Publications, Inc.
5674 Shattuck Avenue
Oakland, CA 94609

Cover design by Amy Shoup
Text design by Michele Waters

ISBN 1-57224-331-7 Paperback

New Harbinger Publications' Web site address: www.newharbinger.com

05    04    03

10    9    8    7    6    5    4    3    2    1

First printing

# Contents

Introduction . . . . . . . . . . . . . . . 1

Says You! . . . . . . . . . . . . . . . 5

Light Your Fire *(Speaking Your True Intention)*  6

Sing It! *(Assertiveness)*  8

PDA Is Not Okay *(Including Everyone)*  10

Now Hear This! *(Getting Their Attention)*  12

Nitty-Gritty *(Appropriate Level of Detail)*  14

The Trusty Switcheroo *(Changing the Subject)*  16

Calling a Safe Time-Out *(Safe Time-Outs)*  18

Wallflowers Anonymous *(Starting Conversations, Speaking Up)*  20

Mind Your Tone! *(Using Tome of Voice)*  22

Um, Like, You Know *(Cutting Down on Fillers)*  24

Know When to Hold 'Em *(Don't Play All Your Cards)*  26

Spill It, Baby *(Deciding When and What to Reveal)*  28

Veggie Talk (No More Bull) *(Meaning What Your Say)*  30

Vacuums Suck *(Consider Your Audience)*  32

Lighten Up *(Lightening the Tone)*  34

Shut It! *(Using Silence)*  36

Don't Bring You Down *(High-Status/Low-Status Behavior)*  38

Giving Props *(Giving and Receiving Compliments)*  40

Take It to the Limit *(Telling a Good Story)*  42

Keep a Lid on It *(Avoiding Excessive Self-Disclosure)*  44

Shock the Monkey *(Spicing Up the Conversation)*  46

Q Give It Up *(Generous Conversation)*   48

Q You Do Know! *(Don't Say "I Don't Know")*   50

Q Walk My Way *(Persuading Others)*   52

Q No Laughing Matter *(Squelching Nervous Laughter)*   54

Q That's the Way I Like It *(Making Statemnts versus Posing Questions)*   56

Q You've Got a Little Something . . . *(Dealing with Others' Physical Faux Pas)*   58

# Say What? . . . . . . . . . . . . . 61

Q Between the Lines *(Listening to What's Said, What's Not Said)*   62

Q What*ever*! *(How to Depersonalize)*   64

Q Thanks for Sharing *(Dealing with Overdisclosure)*   66

Q Get Outta There! *(Disengaging from Bad Conversation)*   68

Q Back on Track *(Combating Conversation Derailers)*   70

Q Blowing Off Blowhards *(Dealing with Egomaniacs and Narcissists)*   72

Q Mum's the Word *(Using Silence)*   74

Q Tears without Fears *(Crying in Social Situations)*   76

Q I Don't Think So *(Contradicting Tactfully)*   78

Q Mind Your Own Beeswax! *(Handling Prying)*   80

Q To the Not-So-Bitter End *(Don't Be Wedded to the Outcome)*   82

# Get into the Groove . . . . . . . . . . . . 85

Q Rock Steady *(Matching Conversational Rhythm)*    86

Q Get a Little Closer *(Deepening Connection)*    88

Q Riff Master *(Riffing Effortlessly)*    90

Q Talk Hog *(Give-and-Take—Gauging Proportions)*    92

Q Pump It Up, Take It Down *(Matching Intensity and Volume)*    94

Q Let's Get Physical *(Reading and Speaking Body Language)*    96

Q Stop, Look, and Listen *(Responding to Indirect Conversational Styles)*    98

Q Work It *(Using Group Dynamics)*    100

Q Wheeler-Dealer *(Negotiating)*    102

Q Loose Lips *(Gossiping Safely)*    104

Q Think It Over *(Don't Respond in the Moment)*    106

Q Don't Try So Hard *(You Don't Have to Say the Perfect Thing)*    108

Introduction

It's happened to all of us: we're in some sort of casual social interaction, chatting up a stranger, and suddenly we find ourselves mired in the muck of social awkwardness. Maybe it's because we've just discovered we're talking to the world's lowest talker ("Um, what was that? I couldn't quite hear you"), or maybe we've just spotted the huge morsel of spinach stuck in the other person's teeth. Or it could be because they've just asked the most outrageous question you could think of ("Yes, actually, they *are* real"). There are so many ways we get stuck in the ghastly, slo-mo reality of social awkwardness and so few tools to get unstuck—until now.

*Talk to Me: Conversation Tips for the Small-Talk Challenged* is your guide to navigating the sometimes-stormy seas of small talk. Here, in one handy-dandy place, are fifty tips, tricks, and strategies to help you shine in any small-talk situation. So many of us know we can be great conversationalists—after all, it's easy when we're with friends. When you're relaxing with the folks you know well, the jokes come flying, the interesting topics sail out, and those bon mots—forget about it! But when we're faced with unfamiliar situations and new people, we're often at a loss. That's because we simply don't know what to expect. We're not yet familiar with the social cues these new folks may use, and we certainly have little idea about their expectations of the situation or us. Even the smoothest chat cat can be nervous when faced with the unfamiliar.

*Talk to Me* is your one-stop guide to prepare you for a potentially nerve-wracking social situation or help you recover from one. We promise never to talk down to you, just to tell it like it is. You can either flip through to find the conversation bugaboos that often trip you up, look up specific situations to prepare for a party you dread, or find explanations and pick-me-ups when you feel you've made a conversational gaffe. We wrote with our tongues firmly in cheek, because as embarrassing, uncomfortable, and sometimes excruciating as small talk can be, no one ever died from it. Remember to give yourself a break, try to learn from every awkward moment, and use *Talk to Me* to help decipher what on earth is going on in the crazy world of small talk. The more confident you feel talking to strangers, the brighter you'll shine at parties, work, and everyday life. You know you can do it! You just need to know the tricks of the trade—and *Talk to Me* will teach you.

# Light Your Fire

There's a lot to be said for speaking your mind. We get so caught up in playing games and trying to seem cool in social situations that we often don't get the chance to actually say what we mean. Sandy is a good example.

Sandy was crazy about Wendy. They'd met through regular hikes with the Sierra Club, and Sandy loved Wendy's bizarre sense of humor and her fantastic travel stories. Sandy really wanted to be closer friends with Wendy but didn't want to come off as a big needy freak. She'd always played it very cool—and still wasn't as close to Wendy as she'd like. At this weekend's hike, she decided that things would be different.

The whole group met up at the trailhead, and Sandy was able to spot Wendy through the masses of Patagonia. "Hey, good to see you again," she said as she sidled up to Wendy. They exchanged how-are-yous and followed the group as they began to head up the trail. Sandy reminded Wendy that she'd promised to tell Sandy about her most recent trip to Africa, and they were off.

By the end of the hike, Sandy had really enjoyed Wendy's company—but hadn't done anything to let Wendy know that she wanted to be closer friends. She was just so used to being reserved, letting others make the first move. But she suspected that Wendy wasn't too assertive on the friendship front, either. Maybe Wendy actually despised Sandy, and that's why she hadn't asked Sandy out for coffee. That was a possibility. But Sandy was sure she'd never find out if she didn't stick her neck out a little and say what she really felt.

As the group reached the end of the hike and folks were standing around saying good-bye, Sandy decided to just do it—go ahead and speak her mind. She took a deep breath and said, "You know, I really want to hear more of your terrific travel stories. These hikes are just too short! I'd love to get together for coffee during the week sometime. What do you think?"

She'd done it! She'd really put herself out there and let her true intentions be known. For a brief moment she felt like one big exposed nerve hanging out in the cold wind. Her heart was beating so hard that she could hardly hear Wendy's reply, which was yes, of course she'd like to hang out. Sandy felt like she'd just scored a winning touchdown as she and Wendy exchanged phone numbers. They've since become great friends.

Most of us would rather hide our true feelings in social situations because we're afraid of being vulnerable. If we let someone know that we really like them, we're nervous that they'll think we're coming on too strong. If we disagree with someone, we're afraid to let them know, even in the most respectful way, because we might come off as wrong or unpleasant. But not speaking from our true intention means that we're not telling it like it is—we're bottling up the truth of how we feel. This is one surefire way to miss out on getting what you want, whether it's gaining a new friend or getting the loudmouth in front of you to stop spewing his ideas in your face. If you communicate with a sense of openness, conviction, compassion, and respect for the other person, you're sure to feel lighter and freer, and end up getting more of what you want in social encounters. Sure it's a risk to show who you really are, but how else is anyone going to know what you need? Go ahead and let them know.

# Sing It!

Most of us are a bit shy sometimes about tellin' it like it is. Whether you're habitually shy or just find yourself tongue-tied in particular situations, you probably know what it feels like to skirt an issue, hoping the other person will somehow divine what you mean to say without your having to come right out with it. We might call this kind of behavior a lack of assertiveness, and it's afflicted us all at one time or another.

Walter often had trouble speaking his mind, especially in social situations. He had been raised to avoid talking about himself and was encouraged not to make a fuss. Today, Walter has a really hard time expressing himself honestly even to his close friends, much less new people. Sometimes this leaves him feeling like everybody's doormat.

What Walter needs is a heaping helping of assertive communication. Speaking assertively means respectfully and clearly saying what you mean. Assertive communication avoids blaming and always makes sure to state things from the speaker's perspective, staying clear of global assertions about what's right or wrong, and instead talking about how the speaker sees and feels about a situation.

When you speak assertively, you express

- what you think about a situation,
- your feelings about the situation, and
- what you want from the situation.

This way your listener will know how you see things, how you feel, and where to go from there. Let's see Walter give it a spin.

There were a lot of folks Walter didn't know at his sister Suzie's birthday dinner party, but he had spotted Laura, the lovely lady he'd been pining over for the past few weeks. He was determined to get to know her a little better at this party—he'd only had small talk with her before. But he saw that he had some competition. Gary, notorious ladies' man that he was, was buzzing around Laura like a bee at a lily, tossing off obnoxious one-liners like some kind of twenty-first-century Don Rickles. Walter doubted that the ordinarily quiet Laura would go for that kind of bluster and knew he could make some headway if he could just get next to her.

When they all sat down for dinner, Walter thought he had it made: he scored a seat right next to Laura. But when he got up to help Suzie get something from the kitchen, he came back to find that Gary had scooted over and was sitting in his chair!

Now, Walter may ordinarily have let this slide. After all, he wasn't the type to make a big scene at a party. But he really liked Laura, and Gary was treating him like some kind of pushover. Well, pushover no longer! Walter took a second to get his eyes on the prize, steel his nerve, then said, "Hey Gary, outta my seat, man." Gary looked up, smiling, and replied "Oh, well, I warmed mine up for you right here." He patted the seat on his other side, but Walter held firm. "Nope, slide it on over. There's a no-seat-stealing policy at Suzie's." He stood there, simply looking at Gary until Gary would have looked like even more of an ass if he didn't move over. Walter sat down and got a big smile from Laura. In fact, she even looked relieved. Risk rewarded!

So, by considering the situation, what he wanted from it, and how he felt, Walter was able to make it clear that he wasn't going to put up with any seat-stealing varmint like Gary. For the rest of the party, he had a great time getting to know Laura. And this time, he didn't go home feeling like a doormat. Quite an improvement, eh?

# PDA Is Not Okay

You've seen it and you've probably done it yourself. You're in a group of people, some of whom you don't really know that well, and you feel uncomfortable. Lucky for you, there is someone you *do* know really well. Maybe it's your love muffin. Maybe it's your best pal. You cling to them for dear life and hope everyone can see just how great your relationship is, and thus just what a good person you are. The two of you refer to your relationship often ("We go *way* back!"), you talk a little louder than everyone else, and maybe you even hang on each other like a drowning victim clings to a life preserver. It's called PDA (public display of affection), and sometimes it can be used for evil instead of for good.

What's the harm in a little affection? Well, none, if the context is right. We're not saying you shouldn't hold hands in public or give your sweetie a smooch or two while you're sitting in the theater before the movie starts. And we're not saying you shouldn't be proud of your close friendships and acknowledge them to others. It's really a matter of context and proportion, and making sure that you're not using PDA to make yourself feel comfortable at the expense of alienating others.

Naomi loved her friends Robert and Myla, but she hated going out to dinner with just the two of them. They'd been married for ten years, and they were still hot for each other. And Naomi was happy for them, really she was. But when they did their tag-team conversation, when they spoke over each other and told stories as a united front, she found it difficult to get a word in edgewise or to connect with either of them personally. They were so into being together that Naomi never felt like there was much room for their being with her. And sometimes, when things were at their worst and Robert and Myla were feeling really lovey-dovey, they'd stop in the middle of their conversation, look into each other's eyes, and give each other a long, slow kiss. Naomi found their behavior perplexing and a tad bit excruciating: "It's not like there's tongue or anything, but it feels creepy all the same. It's like counting lightning: One one thousand, two one thousand, three one thousand, *crash!* And then I'm just sitting there, watching them bask in the glow of their love, not sure if I'm supposed to watch them kiss for what feels like several minutes but is probably ten seconds, or if I'm supposed to look away and give them their privacy. Except that they're not in private, they're hanging out with me!"

If you feel nervous in social situations, or you're simply more comfortable with one person than the others, it can be tempting to focus most of your attention on the person you know best. It may take the form of excessive touching or constant dueling-banjos storytelling, or maybe even incessant teasing. You may not even be aware that you're doing it, but sticking to someone like glue keeps others from being able to find a point of contact with you.

If you suspect that you indulge in excessive PDA, consider trying the following:

- **Try sitting apart.** At dinner parties, sit next to someone other than your spouse if you know either of you tends to be particularly shy or show-offy. The temptation to spend the evening talking to each other might be too strong for you to overcome. At bigger events, make sure you spend at least some time mingling separately.

- **Self-monitor.** Share only one or two stories about your loved one with the group. Remember to ask others questions about themselves. Keep focused on making new connections and on functioning as your own person, not as part of a unit.

# Now Hear This!

Hot dog! Peter had finally scored an invitation to hang out with "the gang," a group of folks from work that was notoriously cliquey and hard to crack. Peter didn't care that much about hanging with the in crowd—he'd had enough of that kind of competition in high school, thank you very much—but there was a particular member of this club who did catch his interest. Now he would finally have a chance to talk to Monica, the new woman in marketing.

Of course, this invitation didn't mean that he'd have an automatic entrée into Monica's heart. In fact, Peter was a little bit worried about having any face time with her at all. Group gatherings generally weren't his best venue to impress. Being naturally shy, he tended to get lost in the shuffle and sometimes ended up feeling like the little brother tagging along for the ride. But not this time! He was going to be the heat-seeking missile of conversation. He'd been working at it, and this time he had the skills to pay the bills.

When Friday evening came, the group of seven folks headed out to McCarthy's Bar down the street from work. At first, Peter felt a little awkward. He didn't have an established place in the group, so he wasn't even sure whom to walk next to. When they got to the bar, there was more awkwardness about where to sit. But Peter had his eye out and managed to score a seat across from Monica at the end of the table.

They started discussing office scuttlebutt, then moved on to the newest Paul Thomas Anderson movie. Peter was able to get a few comments in, but he still hadn't really engaged Monica like he wanted to. It wasn't until they were all standing outside the bar, getting ready to go their separate ways, that Peter made his move. He made sure to make eye contact with Monica, as he had done throughout the evening, smiled directly at her, and asked her how she liked her new job. The other folks, who knew Monica better and had heard the story, talked amongst themselves while Monica gave Peter her impressions of the work scene. As they all walked to their cars, he and Monica continued talking. Peter thought "Hee haw, I've done it. The ice is officially broken." On Monday, he was able to strike up a conversation with her much more easily.

How did Peter manage to shatter that iceberg? Well, aside from being generally nice and trying not to pant or drool, he used some basic attention-getting tricks. That's right, there's no need to learn to juggle or wear a large feathered headdress to grab people's attention. Just try these basic strategies:

- **Make eye contact.** This is basic good communication, but it's especially important if you want someone's attention. Catch the person's eyes and flash a smile. This way you're letting them know that you're interested. Once you've got their eyes on you, that's when you start talking.

- **Try a little touch.** Okay, now we're not suggesting that you go ahead and cop a feel. Not advisable. But, if it won't be too awkward or forced (better if you're positioned close to the person rather than having to make a long-distance grab), a light touch on the arm can make them look your way—at which point you dazzle them with the ol' eye contact and smile.

- **Ask a question.** Offer the other person a chance to talk about what they're doing or how they feel about something pertinent. It's often easier for folks to talk about themselves—after all, they probably know the material. So give them this easy way to make a connection with you. This, coupled with the eye contact and dazzling smile, will help you come across as interested—and interesting. Voilà! Ice shattered.

# Nitty-Gritty

Quantity isn't always quality. The Hunka Hungry Man dinner special at the local steak house is likely to have more fat and gristle than you care to encounter, whereas the Fit and Trim Health Nut dinner likely has just about the same amount of edible meat, with all unappealing extras trimmed away. Clever party conversation is the same: it's better to trim away the fat instead of mucking your story up with extraneous details.

When Jacob goes to dinner parties, he always feels uncomfortable. All those fussy courses, unfamiliar utensils, and endless opportunities for awkward silences. His boyfriend, Wes, charms everyone with clever stories and witty banter, and Jacob desperately wants to hold up his end of the conversation, but he senses that he never gets it quite right.

Finally, after another evening when Wes's stories made everyone laugh and his stories made everyone at the table smile that strained smile that always accompanies glazed eyes, Jacob decided that he needed to know what was going on. As he and Wes were driving home, he said, "Okay. Tell me what it is I'm doing wrong. Why am I such a dreadful party person?"

Wes made a sympathetic grimace, keeping his eyes glued to the road. "Oh, I wouldn't go that far. You know everyone loves you."

"Yeah, yeah, they love me. But they all looked like they were looking around for the emergency exit as soon as I started telling that story about my hernia. You always tell your story about getting your stomach pumped after we ate those iffy enchiladas, and everyone loves it. Why do my stories suck? I need to know." Jacob was truly perplexed.

"Well, it's about *how much* you tell, and how you tell it," Wes explained, figuring that even if the truth hurt, it was better to tell it fast and straight. "I mean, I love your hernia story, and it could be a party pleaser, but then you start telling way too many details about the nurse's family problems and calling in sick and getting behind at work, and it gets kind of . . . well, honestly, it gets a little boring. And you might want to save it until *after* dinner, 'cause it's kind of gross to think about innards poking through your flesh while you're eating a spaghetti dinner. I mean, it's just a suggestion . . ."

While Jacob was a bit embarrassed to hear confirmation that his stories were dragging out and everyone was bored stiff, he was relieved to get a chance to try a new approach. With Wes's help, he was able to learn how to tell a better story, and dinner parties started to seem enjoyable. (Though he still hates those little baby forks!)

If you've ever been on the receiving end of TMI (too much information), you know how dreadful it can be. The person just keeps going on and on about something you couldn't care less about or, even worse, something that seems way too personal. Following are some things to keep in mind:

- **Always consider your surroundings.** If you're at a mingling party, don't tell long involved stories. Just pick the one that's most relevant to the conversation or the situation and leave it at that (unless the person asks you more). You can go into more depth at a dinner party or a longer event, but you still want to trim the fat and give them your best details.

- **Take cues from others.** When in doubt, it's always a good idea to see how much detail others are going into and try to roughly match that.

- **Know when to get out.** If people start to look glazed over, wrap it up.

# The Trusty Switcheroo

Have you ever found yourself stuck in a conversation you'd really rather not have? It's not the person you're talking to, it's just that you've gotten mired in some uninteresting, uncomfortable, or downright distasteful topic. How can you steer the conversation your way?

Todd could not believe he was back in this situation: standing across from Paul, listening to one of Paul's tales of gastric distress. Todd had had some great conversations with Paul in the past—they shared an interest in skiing, leftist politics, and Provence—but Paul sometimes got on this very corporeal kick and, frankly, it made Todd a little ill.

"Oh, lemme tell ya, I don't know why I continue to eat burritos. Whew! Do they repeat on me. I mean, all night long, I'm back in jalapeño land! Oh, and let me tell you what happened at three this morning . . ."

"God save me," thought Todd. He knew some disgusting bathroom episode would follow. How could he avoid hearing this story without making Paul feel bad? After all, he did want to talk to Paul—just not about what happened to him in the can.

"Hold on there, hombre! Maybe we could save the rest of this story for after the buffet. What I really wanted to ask you about was Aspen. How was the skiing, man?"

Paul laughed, suddenly realizing that buffet-time at a party perhaps wasn't the perfect place for his burrito story. Because Todd was obviously interested in talking to him—just not about his irritable bowel—he was happy to move to another story.

Changing the subject smoothly and considerately takes practice, but it's the perfect alternative to abandoning a conversation with someone you like. Even if you're stuck talking to a person you'd rather skip, changing the subject can help alleviate your suffering until you can make your getaway. Can't face discussing your best friend's faults with his tedious girlfriend? Try the handy switcheroo!

- Remember that you have a right to decide what you do and don't want to talk about. Changing the subject may seem a little sneaky at first, but it will allow you to exercise this right without offending anyone or having to end a conversation entirely.

- The person you're talking to probably doesn't realize that their chosen topic is less than attractive to you, so avoid being insulting about it. "I can't believe you're crass enough to bring up politics here" will be less effective and more troublesome than "You know, I'm getting really tuckered from all the political talk lately. Has anyone seen that new reality show *Beauty Parlor Brawls?*"

- The most effective way to change the subject is to own it. In other words, use the word "I" when you switch: "Oh, that's a great story, but what I really want to know is how you got out of that cave in Guatemala" or "I'm really sorry about all the surgery you've been telling us about, but I'm curious to know how your nephew's doing in the Air Force." Using "I" makes your request personal and very hard to refuse.

- It's best to switch to something that still indicates your interest in the other person. In effect, you want to let them know that you're not trying to shut them up, only asking them to consider another subject. Try to find something about the person that you're interested in, and ask about that. You can ask about a mutual friend, an experience they've had, or even their opinion about some current event. Changing the subject by focusing on them will ease the transition and let them know it's not personal.

Make sure to practice your switcheroo skills—they'll only get smoother with use.

# Calling a Safe Time-Out

We've all been caught in conversations that we'd rather ditch—those times when a trip to the bathroom seems to be the only way out. But what about when you're actually enjoying the conversation and you really *do* have to visit the head? How can you get the brief break you need while letting the other person know that you aren't blowing them off? It's all a matter of being open and clear.

The minute the front door opened, Joanie started scanning the group for Lana. Joanie had been psyched to attend the writers' brunch that morning because she'd heard that Lana, a writer at Joanie's favorite alternative music magazine, would be there. Lana was notoriously shy and had so far managed to avoid all the local writers' functions Joanie had attended. But this time Joanie was in full Ahab mode—her white whale would not escape!

After a half hour of subtle trolling (and two mimosas to help get her nerve up), Joanie finally found Lana alone in the kitchen. Joy of joys, Joanie had her! They were actually having a great conversation, with Lana opening up and Joanie feeling almost ready to hit her up for help in her freelance career. But Joanie was starting to regret those mimosas, which had seemingly gone right through her. She was beginning to be distracted by her almost overwhelming need to visit the facilities—but she didn't want to let Lana go just when she was making some headway.

"This is getting ridiculous," thought Joanie as she gave Lana another distracted, gritted-teeth smile. "I've just gotta go." She waited for a pause in what Lana was saying and made her bid: "Lana, I'm really, really enjoying talking to you, and I want to continue this conversation, but I've gotta take a bathroom break. Can I find you in five minutes?"

Even though Lana's shyness sometimes made her hear rejection where none existed, this time she felt very clear that Joanie actually did want to continue the conversation. She laughed, raised her glass, and said, "Sure! I'll meet you out on the patio."

Sometimes it's hard to tell someone you just met how you're really feeling about them without sounding like you're either coming on too strong ("Though I suspect we'll soon be best friends, I desperately need a brief hiatus") or being too coy ("Yeah, like, whatever . . . I gotta pee"). The key, as with so much communication, is being honest, clear, and direct. Doing so is important, though it means tipping your hand and showing your feelings. This may feel a bit awkward at first, but it's the best way to let the person know what you want. Try these steps for taking a safe time-out:

- **Be honest.** Start out by letting your conversation partner know how much you're enjoying the conversation and how valuable it is to you ("I'm really loving talking to you like this" or maybe "You know, this is the best conversation I've had at the party so far").

- **Be clear.** After laying the groundwork, it's safe to explain that you need to take a break. It helps if you can tell your partner why ("I need to use the facilities" or "I promised the baby-sitter I'd call her by 11:00"), though it's not essential if the reason is too complicated.

- **Be direct.** Let them know that you want to continue talking when you return and offer a specific time ("Can I hook up with you again in ten minutes?"). This strategy tells the person that you're serious and lets them know how long they might expect to be in limbo.

Taking a time-out is made safe when you also take the opportunity to be honest, clear, and direct about how you feel and what you want.

# Wallflowers Anonymous

Sometimes the hardest thing about communication is getting it started. If you've ever hung back, blending into the wallpaper, know that you're not alone. All of us feel shy at times. The key is to use some simple strategies to bust that ice wide open.

Nibbling on his mini quiche, Shane eyed the group clustered around the fireplace. He knew he didn't want to hover around the food table any longer and felt that now was the time to try and make contact with other folks at the party. Having just moved to town, he'd come to his brother's shindig specifically to meet some people, but he was feeling the familiar, chilly tentacles of shyness threatening to pull him back.

Well, tentacles be damned! He had spent a good hour thinking about this party and how he wanted to behave. He was sick of feeling lonely, and he had made a firm decision to try to put himself out there, taking a risk in order to open his world a bit. And now was the time to strike.

First he took his emotional temperature for a moment. Yes, he was a bit nervous, a little afraid of being rejected. But, he reminded himself, most people feel nervous in a social situation like this, and besides, it really wouldn't be the end of the world if he were rejected. He could just try again with another person. He reminded himself to keep his body language open and welcoming—no crossed arms or darting eyes. And off he went!

Ambling slowly toward the fireplace group, Shane listened to what they were saying. Apparently they were discussing the local real estate market. Okay! Shane definitely knew something about that. He went up and stood a bit apart. When he heard one woman say, "I just don't know where people are buying these days, prices are so steep," Shane grabbed the opportunity. "I just bought in Oak Hills. There are still some great deals there." The woman who had spoken smiled and nodded at him, the group opened a bit to allow him in, and suddenly he was talking!

Most people can find it hard to break into a group or talk to strangers, whether at a party, at work, or even on the bus. The first step to overcoming your feelings of shyness is to forgive yourself for them—we all have them. Next, you can implement these very simple, practical strategies for breaking the ice. Soon you'll be the life of the party!

- When you're gearing up to make a new connection, take a moment to determine how you're feeling. Is your body tense? If so, take a deep breath and try to relax a bit. Are you telling yourself that you're sure to get rejected? If you are, try replacing that thought with something more positive, like "Maybe I'll have a nice conversation" or "Maybe I'll like them."

- Recognize and give yourself a break for any fears of rejection you may be entertaining. Remind yourself that getting rejected will not kill you, and you'll always get another chance with someone else, even if you do get the brush-off.

- Keep your body language in mind. If you want to break into a group of people, stand fairly near it. Talking at them from the side of the room won't give them the opportunity to include you, no matter how safe it may feel. When talking one-on-one, make sure your body is open, your facial expressions reflect your responses, and that you make eye contact with whoever is speaking.

- If you're stuck for something to say, keep these tips in mind: bringing up similarities or differences, talking about current events, offering a compliment, and using humor all work wonders in opening up the conversation.

Take these techniques out for a spin and see if you don't become the Chatty Cathy you've always wanted to be!

# Mind Your Tone!

The tone with which you speak can say a lot about how you're feeling and who you are. That's why considering your tone of voice can be crucial to communication success.

Pico arrived at his hotel hot, tired, and cranky about the long flight he'd just endured. It didn't help that his room in the hotel turned out to be dark, tiny, and over the garage. Sheesh! He was only visiting Georgia in the sweltering heat of August to attend an important business conference. Now he felt like maybe the trip was a big mistake.

After a claustrophobic night spent waking up to cars speeding into the garage below and an air conditioner that worked only intermittently, Pico dragged himself to the conference. His stomach felt like a kettle on high heat, boiling away with the anger he felt about his miserable night. But it looked like his luck was changing when he spied Alice Samson emerging from a conference room. Alice was the new big marketing guru, and Pico, who had met her briefly a few times, had wanted to reconnect.

"Alice!" Pico called out. Alice smiled and walked over, and the two began to talk. Alice was in a jovial mood and started telling Pico a funny story about running into an old flame, which Pico ordinarily would have found hilarious. But he was still seething from the night before. He knew he needed to watch it when he burst out with a loud, harsh laugh at one of the funnier bits in the story, a laugh so explosive and hostile it made Alice stop and blink. As she continued her story, Pico reminded himself that talking to Alice was more important to him than expressing his anger, and also that he'd really rather enjoy her story than feel angry. He concentrated on what she was saying and kept his voice light and easy, soon discovering that he was actually feeling better. He was laughing naturally and really hitting it off with Alice.

Because he'd matched her tone, she felt appreciated and respected, and the two went on to have a profitable (and enjoyable) business meeting.

Keeping your tone of voice appropriate to the conversation is a matter of sensitivity and conversational practicality. When your tone slips too far away from your partner's, you give the impression that you don't really care about how your partner is feeling or necessarily even want to be involved in the conversation. Matching tone doesn't mean pretending to feel something that you don't; it simply means remaining sensitive to the level and tone of the conversation and compromising to assure the comfort of those you're talking with. It's a way of listening to your conversational partner and responding in kind.

Tone is about the sound of your voice as well as what you say. For example, it's probably best to keep your voice smooth and moderately pitched in most conversations. Slipping into a harsh, angry, or highly upset tone is really only appropriate with close friends.

Consider how you would like your partner to sound if the tables were turned. For example, if you were upset by a family problem, wouldn't you want the other person's voice to be soft, smooth, and caring? If you were sharing what you thought was a hilarious joke, wouldn't you want the other person's tone to be light?

Keeping your voice in medium to lower registers and relatively calm are good rules of thumb in most conversations. Most folks would rather hear a smooth, evenly toned voice than one that rises to shrieks or fades away in basement-level mumbles.

# Um, Like, You Know

Um, fillers, fillers, and, like, fillers. You know what we mean?

When we're chatting with strangers, we want them to think we're fabulously witty, smart, and interesting. And yet many of us have this annoying little habit of cluttering up our words with a bunch of garbage that makes us sound like Sean Penn's surfer dude character in *Fast Times at Ridgemont High*. And this is, like, totally not cool.

Aaron was clueless that he said "you know?" at the end of every other sentence. It wasn't until he went to a career counselor who was kind enough to point it out that he became aware of the problem. And once he noticed it in himself, he couldn't help but notice it in everyone else. One of his friends said "um" before answering even the easiest of questions. His brother said "like" way too often. And, Aaron had to admit, these things made them sound much less intelligent than they really were.

Are you a victim of conversation fillers? If you're not sure, ask a friend or two to monitor you in a few social situations. For instance, have them hang out with you at a party, and, while you're chatting away with others, see if they can identify any culprits.

Aaron had his girlfriend listen for fillers at a dinner party they went to together. At first he was a little self-conscious about knowing he was being "tested," but after a while he just eased into his normal conversation style. At the end of the evening, in the car driving home, his girlfriend shook her head in disbelief. "Not only did *you* say 'like' and 'you know' like a thousand times, but did you notice how often George and Ben say 'um?' And I noticed myself doing it, too. It's incredible how lame we all sound."

If it's time for a little "filler buster" action, the first thing to do is notice which words you add in the most often. Some frequent fillers are "um," "like," "you know," "uh," "hmm," "I don't know," "I mean," "well," "blah blah blah," "yadda yadda yadda," and "et cetera et cetera et cetera."

Once you know what you're working with, you need to commit yourself to reducing your fillers over time. The first way to do this is simply to work on noticing it yourself. Don't beat yourself up when you say it, just take note when you do and try to avoid it the next time. It may make you a bit awkward during the transition, but after a few weeks you'll get back to your normal conversation, without those burdensome fillers.

The other thing you can do is make a "filler buster" pact with a few friends. Call each other on your fillers when they slip out in conversation. After a while, you'll get used to not using them.

And what do you use to replace fillers? Every conversation has lulls, and sometimes you need to buy yourself a few seconds to think. Here are a few fillers that, used sparingly, will make you sound more thoughtful instead of less so:

- That's interesting.
- I've never thought of that.
- That's a great point.
- Right.
- Yes.

Notice that all of these are communicating something positive, instead of communicating nothing at all. And, in a pinch, feel free to use a few seconds of silence. Nod your head or cock it to the side to indicate that you're thinking about your response, and wait until you really have something to say before you say it.

# Know When to Hold 'Em

Sometimes Nosy Nellies seem to be everywhere, bumping up against your personal business and trying to peer in. When you run into someone who wants to know too much, too soon, one of the best ways to throw them off track is to throw up a roadblock.

Kenya spied her husband, Toby, at the buffet across the room, loading up on sushi. She smiled and moved to join him. They'd been married for about three years now and were starting to think about kids. Kenya had talked about it with some of her girlfriends—and apparently the news was too hot to hold.

As Kenya was getting her share of the California roll, she suddenly looked up to see Denise standing next to her. Denise was a new friend of one of Kenya's oldest buddies from school, though Kenya couldn't, for the life of her, understand what her friend saw in this tiny, bespectacled, and very nosy woman. As a rule, Kenya tried to avoid her—but now she was caught.

"Hey Kenya, hey Toby. I see you're not shy about sushi!" Denise peered up at them, pushing up her heavy glasses. Before Kenya could reply, Denise launched her conversational missile. "So, I hear you guys are trying to get pregnant. How's it going?"

Ugh. Well, there was a good reason she tried to stay away from Denise: her constant prying. Kenya and Toby hadn't even told their parents about the kid thing, and here was this person she barely knew, prodding her about it. Kenya stopped herself from replying with a huffy "None of your business" and hauling Toby away. No, she didn't want to be rude to her friend's unfortunate acquaintance. So she decided to throw this bloodhound off the track.

Kenya smiled and said, "You know, with what I read in the paper this morning, I can't even think about babies. Did you read what the president is saying about NATO?" Kenya proceeded to go on a mini rant about the state of foreign affairs, and by the time she was done, it would have taken an incredible act of will for Denise to drag the conversation back to babies. Mission accomplished!

Throwing up roadblocks is more aggressive than simply changing the subject. A roadblock is intended to obfuscate the conversation, to *force* it to move in another direction, so that the other person would really, really have to push to come back to their question. Most folks, even the nosiest, won't be quite ballsy enough to push past a roadblock.

Here are some roadblock options for your next nosy encounter:

- **Try a joke.** When someone's pushing you in a personal direction, say, "You know, that reminds me of the two penguins on an ice floe." Enthusiastically telling a joke—no matter how silly or unrelated—will "sell" the roadblock, making it very hard for the Nosy Nellie to jump over it.

- **Throw them a cliché.** This is pretty clear code that you don't want to talk about the subject at hand. If Kenya had responded with a "Well, you don't want to count your chickens before they're hatched," Denise might have been a bit bewildered, but she'd have had a hard time getting back to the baby question. If she did, Kenya could use one of the other techniques as a one-two punch.

- **Radically change the subject.** Again, when you try this one, you need to really sell it. Putting your feelings into it will make it seem rude to go back to the original question. After all, you *really want* to talk about this new subject. The other person would really have to strain to get you off of it.

Though these may feel a little awkward at first, remember that you're trying to tell the nosy person where to get off—without being rude. These strategies are only as artificial as the situation you're trying to squeeze out of. So go at them with gusto!

# Spill It, Baby

Cici was bored by her day job as a corporate executive, so she decided to take a night class at the local university. She loved writing in her private journal, and she knew she had some pretty intense stories to tell, so she signed herself up for a memoir-writing class.

First thing on Monday night, her instructor had everyone go around in a circle and share the topics they were planning to write about in the class. Now, Cici knew that she wanted to write about being sexually harassed by her boss, whom she still worked for, but she suddenly felt like hiding under her desk. She couldn't tell these strangers about her personal experiences! She didn't know them from Adam!

Being the lucky girl that she was, she was asked to go first. She decided to try the old corporate soft pedal. "Oh, I'm going to be writing about corporate America."

"That's great," the instructor said, "but memoirs have a very personal element to them. What about *your* experiences in corporate America are you hoping to focus on?"

"Oh, this and that. You know, what it's like to be a woman in a man's world. Polices and such," Cici said, looking absently at her watch.

"Could you be a bit more specific? After all, we're all going to be reading your work in the near future. Don't be shy."

But Cici couldn't do it. After several rounds of this back-and-forth, with Cici still circling around the issue, her instructor moved on to the next person. It was a man who said, "I'm planning on writing about my childhood experiences with sexual abuse, and how I've worked to overcome the stereotypes people have about men and those experiences."

At first, Cici was shocked by his candidness, until she saw that everyone else was discussing similarly painful topics. In this setting, she realized, she should have just revealed a bit of her private life. After all, didn't she hope that strangers would eventually read about these very same experiences when she published her memoir and became a stunningly famous writer? And she already knew who she wanted to play her in the movie adaptation . . .

So how do you know when spilling the beans will drive people away and when it will show them that you aren't some secretive mystery person with heavy baggage and something to hide? The trick to knowing when and what to reveal is to observe those around you and consider the setting. In group therapy, you share intimate details from the get-go. At a party, it's better to wait and see how open others are being, and only reveal what seems appropriate and comfortable to you.

It's especially important to consider the level of detail you should go into in any given conversation. For instance, the man in Cici's class was honest and forthcoming, but he saved the specifics for his writing and shared his topic calmly, without tears or drama. He understood the difference between a writing class, where it is important to reveal the truth, and a therapy session, where it is important to feel your feelings about the truth.

While it's generally a good idea to refrain from revealing intimate details to strangers or people you've just met, there are occasions when this is actually appropriate, and not doing so separates you from the group. Consider your surroundings and the purpose of being there, and let the behavior of others help guide you in deciding how much to share.

# Veggie Talk (No More Bull)

If you're prone to exaggerate or you always have to put a positive spin on everything, it may be time to cut the bull and switch over to 100 percent organic, wholesome veggie talk. It's better for your health to get real, and it's better for connecting with others as well. When people sense that you're not being real with them, it can be hard for them to get to know you.

Mary Jane was raised to never complain. If she had an awful bout of the flu and someone tried to offer sympathy, she'd just say, "Oh, no! I'm fine. At least it's not tuberculosis." When she was laid off from her job, she insisted to everyone that it must be for the best, and she kept her anxieties to herself. And when she told stories, she embellished nearly to the point of lying: she was laughing *hysterically* with her coworkers, it was the *funniest* thing she'd ever seen in her life, she'd had the *greatest* time of her life (every single weekend).

Her attempts to put a positive spin on things felt phony to everyone else. Even her close friends weren't sure what she was really thinking or feeling most of the time, and when she told them stories, they knew that she was likely building it up to be more than it really was. Sometimes they'd ask her how she really felt about things, but she'd just bat her eyelashes and insist that everything was going just great.

Mary Jane's excessive efforts to convey a pleasant and positive demeanor were really working against her. She had built such a façade that no one, not even her husband, really knew where her exaggerations ended and the truth began.

It's great to be positive and friendly, especially when you're making small talk with people you've just met or with casual acquaintances. It's generally not a good idea to unload your darkest troubles on someone you barely know. And it's also true that the art of telling a captivating story is in pulling out the best details and making them shine. But good communication is all about subtlety and finesse.

If you know that you tend to exaggerate, consider the following:

- **Rein yourself in.** Try to be aware of the difference between colorful story-telling and outright lying. If something didn't happen, don't add it in to spice things up. If you enjoyed a nice laugh, don't feel like you have to say it was hysterical. When you use extremes as a matter of course, even a few times in a conversation with a stranger, people will pick up on that and begin to suspect that you're disingenuous.

- **Don't be afraid to get real.** It's possible to be both honest and positive in virtually any situation. If you're in the middle of a nasty breakup, you don't have to say, "Oh, well, it's all for the best. Who needs 'em, anyway!" Instead, you can say, "Yes, it's pretty hard right now. But I'm managing to get a lot of support and I can see the light at the end of the tunnel."

Make a connection. Even in casual chitchat with people you've never met before and will likely never see again, the goal is to get to know each other a bit and find some point of connection if at all possible. Making things up or being dishonest defeats the purpose. Being friendly and realistic leaves people with a better impression.

# Vacuums Suck

Jeff had always prided himself on being outspoken, unafraid to voice his opinion to anyone. He also considered himself to be a pretty funny guy, able to turn a phrase in such an outrageous way that he always got a laugh. Well, maybe not always. He'd been meeting a lot of new people lately, and some of his opinions—or maybe the way he was putting them across—weren't going over so well with folks who didn't know him. Sometimes he'd be off on a really great rant and the person he was talking to would head for the bathroom and never return. Jeff was beginning to wonder if he was having hygiene issues. Bad breath? BO? He didn't realize that he was interacting with people as though he were living in a vacuum.

Only last Saturday he was at a little cocktail party meeting some of his new girlfriend's crowd when he got a major cold shoulder from one guy. He was talking about his latest trip to the doctor—he'd gotten that awful flu bug that had been going around—and he took the opportunity to really go off on the medical profession. "Then, after keeping me waiting for, like, a half hour, the doctor breezes in and spends maybe two minutes with me. Sheesh! Well, you know doctors—they're all in it for the money. That guy probably figured he could make a good fifty bucks a minute on me if he kept it short. Greedy bastards, all of 'em."

The guy he was talking to fixed him with a cool look and said, "Well, maybe your doctor is in it for the money, but not all of them are. In fact, my mom is a doctor—a pretty good one. She works with Doctors without Borders helping out in war zones around the world. She actually took a bullet in the arm last year. Now, if you'll excuse me, I need to find my wife."

Oops. Jeff's face was burning and he felt strangely rooted to the floor. He wondered whether the word "idiot" was actually printed on his forehead or it just felt that way. This had been happening to him a lot lately, and he was starting to wonder how many feet he could fit into his mouth at once. He decided then and there that he needed to spend less time trying to be clever and more considering who he was talking to.

All of us have experienced the bitter taste of shoe leather, foot firmly wedged in mouth. It's not pleasant and can alienate you from potential social connections. But how can you know what's going to offend?

Pay attention to your audience. Remember, when you're meeting new people, you never know who you're talking to. No matter what they look like or in what context you meet them, you can never be sure where they're coming from until they let you know. So listen to them and hold off on your fiery opinions or biased assumptions until you get a sense about who they are. Here are some quick tips to keep in mind:

- **When venturing opinions with someone you don't know well, start out gently.** Even if you feel very strongly, ease into expressing your feelings.

- **Listen to how they reply.** If they give you the "Right on!" you probably won't offend them by turning up the intensity. If they demur, watch your step.

- **Be sensitive and respectful.** You can't know the person's life experience or why they hold certain opinions, so try not to judge them if they disagree with you. Be aware that they have a right to their feelings, just as you have to yours. If they disagree with you, that's not a sign to go pit bull on them, attacking without letup.

- **Remember that certain subjects are naturally more touchy than others.** Venturing a strong opinion about the latest John Woo movie is probably less risky than attacking a political party, for instance.

# Lighten Up

Jayne had been single for two years, and she was taking a bit of time to play the field. She liked the rush of the first date: getting dolled up in her favorite clothes, having that jittery feeling in her stomach, wondering what the evening might bring. This is not to say she hadn't had her share of nightmare encounters.

Zach was the worst. A mutual acquaintance had set them up, so they met at a local bar to chat and get to know each other. Halfway into their first drink, Zach started revealing all kinds of overly personal information that was inappropriate for a first date. "Yeah, my dad was a pretty abusive alcoholic. I guess that's why I'm such a careful drinker. Two is my limit. Because in college, I was a real binger. I even had a DUI, and I missed one of my finals because I was in jail. Whew! I gotta watch myself!"

Now, Jayne wasn't the judgmental type. It wasn't that she would automatically discount a potential partner for having a rocky past, but his immediate disclosure of personal information let her know that he wasn't dealing with his issues all that well. And she didn't feel like getting into a stranger's deepest wounds on their first meeting. So she tried to lighten up the conversation, without making it too obvious. "So, where did you go to college?"

"Uh! I went to State. I mean, I should have gone to a better school, but I needed to stay and help my mom deal with her divorce, and, believe me, it wasn't pretty," Zach said, not at all clueing in to Jayne's attempt to shift to your average small-talk topics.

"That's too bad," Jayne tried again. "I loved the state university back home."

Notice how Jayne tried to shift the conversation to herself this time, and she opened the door for Zach to ask her more about the topics she brought up: Where is "home"? What did she enjoy about the school there? What does she do for a living now?

Unfortunately, Zach didn't have the skills to pay the bills. He forgot to ask her a thing about herself, but he did unload more details about his incarcerated sibling and about how much he hated his job. Needless to say, Jayne didn't go out on a second date.

If Jayne's tactics are too subtle for your conversational partner, you can take a more direct approach to try to lighten up a conversation that's going over to the dark side.

- "Wow! This is getting a bit heavy. What say we chat about something a little more fun. What's the last movie you saw?"

- "That sounds hard. But enough of that for now. Tell me about something you do enjoy. Have you ever tried skydiving?"

# Flip Tip

When you're meeting someone new, you want to keep the tone of the conversation lighter and more positive. You don't have to lie—just steer the conversation toward topics you can be enthusiastic about. Hate your job? Mention that you're looking for something new, but shift the focus onto your favorite hobby. Have a troubled past? If someone asks you directly about it, you can say something like, "I had a difficult relationship with my dad growing up, so we're not close now. But I do enjoy a close relationship with my mom." Don't make Zach's mistake of dumping all your awful truths on a stranger you've just met. You have to build a relationship and establish trust before it's appropriate to air your dirty laundry.

# Shut It!

Sometimes the best forms of communication have nothing to do with talking. Keeping your lips sealed can say a lot about how you feel and where you think the conversation is going. In fact, using silence is one of the best ways we know to let your conversational partner know that something big is up.

Marta had been dreading this little get-together for weeks, and now here she was at her grandmother's annual spring soiree. Marta loved most of her grandma's friends, but she also knew that old Charlie—notorious lech and out-of-touch senior of the year—was probably going to show up. Charlie seemed to think it the height of charm to blatantly ogle any woman he chose, something that the older women of his set seemed willing to overlook, but which really drove Marta nuts.

"And here we go," Marta thought as she saw Charlie round the corner and head toward her. His plaid pants were so loud, she wished she'd brought earplugs, but her grandma didn't seem to notice. "Hey hey, here are some lovely ladies!" The women in the small group Marta was standing with smiled indulgently, though Marta did see a couple of them surreptitiously slip away. Why didn't she think of that? Oh well, too late now. "Well, it's good to see *you*, Marta! It's great to get some young blood involved." Marta pasted on a small smile and said, "Thanks, Charlie. I was just talking to Betty here about the new art teacher at the senior center. She says he's giving a great drawing class." Charlie responded with a smirk. "Well, I've got all the art I need right here. Marta, you're a Michelangelo in that blouse. Whooey! I do love fitting clothes on a young girl. But then, I always have been a real boob man."

Boob man. Boob man?! Marta felt her cheeks flame and saw the whole little group take a surprised gulp of air. Oh no, this wasn't going to fly. Marta didn't even know what to say to this creepy dinosaur—so she said nothing. She fixed Charlie (his toothy smile noticeably faltering) with a silent, piercing stare for about four seconds, then moved on. "So, tell me, Grandma, are you taking drawing classes with Betty?" Eventually Charlie slunk away, realizing for once that maybe he needed to be a bit more careful.

When someone goes too far, you probably wish you had just the right remark to throw back at them. You may even have a deep desire to do them bodily harm. But remember that sometimes the strongest statement you can make is no statement at all. Silence lets the other person know that you're not willing to participate. Without saying a word, you lob the ball firmly back into their court, letting them take responsibility for what they've said. Silence used in this way can help you take a powerful stand, refusing to dignify an inappropriate statement with a reply.

Silence is best used in situations where speaking your mind may not be in your best interest. These include conversations with people who have power over you (coworkers, in-laws) and with people who have very little impact on your life.

If you want to use silence powerfully, make sure to maintain eye contact. If you prefer to use it as a passive technique (say, to avoid engaging with your racist father-in-law in a discussion on race), you may want to avoid making eye contact. In this latter case, you're using silence more to play dead than to register disapproval.

Avoid using silence with those close to you. Your intimates deserve the respect of an answer, even if it's one they may not necessarily like. In the end, open communication with your close friends and family is always more important than simply making a point.

# Don't Bring You Down

One thing you certainly want to avoid in any conversation is shooting yourself in the foot by coming off as timid, shy, or unimportant. One way many folks make this mistake is by unconsciously slipping into *low-status behavior,* or ways of behaving that announce to the other person that you may not think much of yourself.

When Deborah got into the car, she was surprised to find a third person. She had been expecting breakfast out with her friend Pauline, but it looked like Pauline had invited a guest.

"Hey Deb, this is the fabulous Marion, my friend in advertising that I've been telling you so much about. I was hoping you two could powwow about the biz, 'cause I think Marion may be able to help you break in."

Deborah smiled and shook Marion's hand, but inside she froze. She didn't feel nearly ready to hobnob with Marion. Schmoozing was one of her least favorite things, and she was caught off guard.

Over her Denver omelette, she found herself clamming up, sitting with her shoulders rounded over, and feeling skittish about making eye contact with Marion. She didn't feel ready to talk to Marion as a peer, so she behaved as if to say, "You're right! I don't know what I'm talking about"—sort of rejecting herself before Marion could.

After breakfast was over and she'd managed to escape any real discussion of her professional goals, Deborah felt rotten. What could she have done differently?

Many of us, when faced with a situation or person we find a bit intimidating, would rather hide out than face the music. We may have the idea that we're really not good enough to handle the situation, and our behavior begins to shift to make us look like we're not worthy. We begin to escape into low-status behavior. Check out some of the low-status actions below to see if you indulge in any of them when you're feeling nervous:

- avoiding eye contact

- letting your shoulders droop or your head dip

- crossing your arms or clenching your arms in front of you

- moving your hands in a fluttery, nervous way, especially in touching your face or hair

- speaking quietly and allowing yourself to be cut off or interrupted

- clenching or twisting your hands

All of these tend to indicate to the person you're talking to that you just might not think much of yourself. In effect, you're ceding the higher-status position to them. This can result in that person feeling uncomfortable, seeing you as uninterested in the conversation, or, at worst, deciding that you can be taken advantage of. Now, you don't want that!

The next time you're faced with a situation or person you find intimidating, try doing the opposite of these low-status behaviors. Take a deep breath and try some high status on for size! Remember to meet the person's gaze, match the volume of their voice (if it's appropriate), and keep your shoulders back and head up. Don't sell yourself short with low-status behavior. Take the credit and respect you deserve by acting like you expect it.

# Giving Props

Knowing how to give and receive compliments with grace is one of the most important keys to successful small talk. Giving appropriate compliments puts people at ease, makes them feel good about themselves, and lets them know that you're trying to be nice to them and get to know them a little better.

Janice was a master at giving compliments. Her mom had once told her that if she thought something nice about someone, she should say it aloud. So if she noticed that someone was wearing a pretty blouse, or that they'd had a haircut, or that they had a great sense of humor, she always made sure she told them.

There are a few tricks to giving compliments:

- Only speak your truth. If you don't like something, don't say you do.

- Give compliments generously, but don't inundate someone. Complimenting a stranger or new acquaintance more than once (or, if absolutely necessary, twice) in a conversation might make them feel like you're making things up just to be nice, or it might make them feel like you're coming on too strong.

- Be tactful. Saying things like, "My, you have beautiful breasts" to someone you just met might be meant as a compliment, but it's unlikely that she'll take it that way. If someone has lost a lot of weight, saying something like, "You look really fantastic" is more appropriate than saying, "Wow! How much weight have you lost?" Some people will offer more details when you open up the conversation, but you want to leave it up to them.

- People like it when you remember something they told you in a previous conversation. Asking a follow-up question ("The last time we talked, you had just started that great new job. How's it going?") is a compliment in the sense that it shows you were listening and paying attention, and that you care what happened.

What if you notice something that you don't particularly like about someone? Do you say something, and if so, what do you say?

In general, if you don't know the person well, or if it doesn't seem like there's anything to be gained from saying it, it's better not to say anything. So, if someone is wearing the loudest, ugliest shirt that's ever seen the light of day, you shouldn't say, "Why, that's an interesting shirt." Just keep your feelings to yourself (and gossip with your friends later if you really have to comment). Likewise, if someone you know gets what you think is a terrible haircut, you should zip your lip. Saying, "Oh, you got your hair cut," without adding, "It looks nice," is simply an insult in disguise. Just like your momma said, if you can't say something nice, don't say anything at all.

# Flip Tip

It's equally important that you receive compliments with kindness and generosity. You always want to say thank you to a well-intentioned and tasteful compliment, even if your own self-esteem level makes it hard for you to believe the truth of the compliment. For instance, while Janice loved to give compliments, she found it hard to accept them herself. While she used to say, "Oh, no!" when someone complimented her, she realized that when people did that to her it really shut down the conversation and made her feel uncomfortable. After that, she always said "thank you," no matter how much it killed her inside. And, as a bonus for her, doing this helped her let in the compliments more over time. It's sort of the fake-it-till-you-make-it approach.

# Take It to the Limit

Who doesn't love a great story? Storytelling has been a tradition since we all lived in caves, and that's because people love to be entertained with a ripping yarn. There are some rules to follow, however. Let's see how Marjorie does with them.

The party started at eight, and Marjorie couldn't wait to get there. She had a truly rock-'em-sock-'em story to tell—for once!—and she wanted to see her friends' faces as they listened with rapt attention. As she drove to the party, she recalled all the bits that made the story great: the free trip to Florida, the grizzled and slightly insane Everglades guy, the alligators, the wrestling with the alligators, the romance with the grizzled Everglades guy. Boy, this story was going to rock!

Cut to an hour later when Marjorie, her friends assembled around her, blew it. What happened? Well, as Marjorie so often does, she started in the middle of the story ("I met this crazy guy in the Everglades—and we got it on!"), gave away delicious details without building suspense ("Yeah, we were eating dinner in his shack, then he had to wrestle the alligator, and we were so full"), and got sidetracked by unimportant details ("You know, the humidity there can really make your hair frizz"). All in all, Marjorie just couldn't seem to get any bang for her buck, even with a potentially great story.

Marjorie always seems to forget the rules of telling a good story. These rules help you set up a rhythm, keying in to the expectations and emotions of the folks listening. Marjorie's scattershot approach disappointed these expectations, leaving her friends confused and a little frustrated ("But why would the guy actually wrestle the alligator?").

The next time you want to wow them with a terrific tale, try these handy dandy tips:

- **Start at the beginning.** Setting up the rhythm of a good story involves laying a foundation for the action ahead. How did you get into this situation? What did you expect would happen? What were the relationships involved? Once your audience knows where you started, they can begin to invest in where you're going to go.

- **Include your feelings.** Simple details, no matter how fantastic, just won't pull in an audience. You need to infuse your story with emotion, describing how the events affected you and the other people involved. When you share your feelings, you give your listeners something to identify with, a dynamic hook to catch hold of. It's the emotions that really make the story come alive.

- **Don't get sidetracked with unnecessary details.** After all, who cares about Marjorie's Florida 'fro? Her listeners wanted to hear about the crazy man and the alligators. Stick to the bits that will move your story along.

- **Build suspense.** Part of laying your foundation is giving tiny clues to what happens next, and you should continue this throughout the story. Marjorie could have started with something like, "When I won my free trip to Florida, I was so excited. After all, I didn't know I'd have to deal with alligators." After that, her listeners will be on tenterhooks, wondering how she had to "deal with" the alligators. Building suspense like this gives the listener a reason to stay interested.

- **Provide an ending.** Stories need a resolution, so don't jump ship after you get all the juicy details out. People will want to know how the events of the story affect you now, how you feel, and what impact has remained. Wrapping it up for them will let them disengage smoothly and leave them feeling satisfied.

Now go forth and wield your storytelling powers responsibly—and gloriously!

# Keep a Lid on It

Have you ever felt compelled to put your worst foot forward? Do you find yourself recounting your entire personal history or your most private details to people you barely know? If so, it's about time you put a lid on it.

Jake had the worst luck on first dates. He dressed nicely, always made it there on time, and tried to be completely open and honest, but he rarely found someone who'd go out with him again. His dates always told him they weren't ready for a relationship, or that they just didn't feel the chemistry, but after hearing that dozens of times, he knew there had to be something that was keeping women from giving him a second chance.

Finally, he decided he had to ask, even if the answer was excruciating. Luckily, his date took pity on him and let him have it: "I'm sure you're a nice person, but I didn't want to hear all about the history of alcoholism in your family *and* your chronic hair-pulling problem on the first date! Maybe if I knew you I could handle that information, but getting it all in the first hour was a bit much."

Jake was a classic case of TMI (too much information), providing his prospective lovers with far more details about his difficulties than his strengths. In his mind, it was best to be totally honest and let women know what they'd be getting themselves into if they dated him. But Jake was mistaking overdisclosure for honesty.

Knowing how much to share with someone, and when, is key to developing relationships with healthy boundaries. It's good to share the deepest parts of yourself with people you know and trust, and that includes talking about your mistakes and insecurities. But if you share too much too soon, you risk scaring people off and making yourself look bad. While there are no hard-and-fast rules about how much to reveal in each situation, it's important to share what feels comfortable to you and to your audience.

Use these guidelines to help gauge the right amount of disclosure in any given situation:

- **Consider your audience.** Telling the checker at the grocery store all about how your partner cheated on you or bombarding your coworkers with the details of your sexual escapades generally isn't appropriate. Sharing these same experiences with close friends, if they express an interest, is a way to deepen your connection. Similarly, telling a prospective employer at a job interview that you sometimes have problems with depression that affect your performance is not a good idea, whereas enlisting the support of your friends and family in this issue would be constructive.

- **Ask and observe.** If you suspect that you're a chronic overdiscloser—unable to keep a secret from anyone, convinced that any amount of privacy is dishonest, or concerned that many people are having a negative reaction to you during conversations—the first thing to do is ask a few people you trust how you are coming off. Use their feedback as a way to assess your behavior and see if it could use some adjustments. Then observe yourself and others in conversation, and note how you feel on both the giving and receiving end.

- **Put your best self forward.** Let people get to know the best parts of you before you share the more challenging parts of your life. Parties, first dates, and other casual social gatherings are places to tell funny stories and raise thought-provoking questions—not to get free therapy.

# Shock the Monkey

It isn't hard to be the life of the party. Here's what you don't do: Never share your detailed preferences for one-ply toilet paper over two, or your deep fondness for lima beans, or why you like one dishwashing detergent over the other. Here's what you do: When you've gotten to know the people you're talking to a bit, and you've made some friendly conversation to lay the groundwork, it's time to take a chance and say something that you know is a risk. Say something risqué or off-color, or take the liberty of teasing someone about something they said.

Vanessa lives a pretty mild-mannered life—secretary by day, sitcom viewer by night. But she does have a great sense of humor, which people often don't expect when they first see her walk in the door in her gray cardigan and casual slacks. But invariably, when she is in a new crowd and the topic of celebrities comes up, she casually throws out, "Well, you know, I once borrowed a tampon from Julia Roberts." That never fails to get attention, and then she tells the whole story about how she ran into Julia in the ladies' room of her favorite restaurant, and they chatted about the cute waiter. Opening with the tampon line is a bit off-color compared to simply saying, "I talked to Julia Roberts at a restaurant once." It's about choosing the most unusual or surprising element of a story and opening with that, instead of with the background.

You can also shock people by responding to what they're saying in a bold way. For instance, once Vanessa was at a party in San Francisco, and a woman she'd been enjoying talking to admitted sheepishly that she'd been hesitant to move to the West Coast because she didn't think that West Coasters were as sharp and funny as East Coasters. Vanessa, a born-and-raised Californian, had already been joking with the woman for a while, so she went ahead and dove in, feigning complete indignation. "That's ridiculous!" she exclaimed in an exaggerated voice. "I'm a West Coaster, and I'm fucking hilarious!" The woman immediately started to laugh. The intensity of Vanessa's tone and language spiced up the conversation in a way that lightened the mood and built a fun connection between them that grew as the evening progressed.

Here are some things to keep in mind when attempting to add some zest:

- **Use these techniques sparingly.** No one wants to feel like you're engaging in a one-person show, spewing jokes and stories without caring what others have to say.

- **Consider your audience and surroundings.** If you're with friends and peers and the party is for adults, it might be okay to share that racy story or that slightly off-color joke. But you wouldn't want to do that at a party where there were children or professional contacts, or where the atmosphere seemed contentedly tame.

- **If you bomb** (people laugh uncomfortably or seem slightly offended), abort! Go back to your polite conversation. Once you've become more practiced and you get better at gauging what works and what doesn't, you can try again later in the evening. When you take conversational risks, sometimes you hit and sometimes you miss. But if you miss repeatedly, you may not get invited back again, so practice a little at a time.

- **Work your way in slowly.** Don't just walk up to a group and start your comedy routine. Start by listening, getting a sense of the conversation, nodding, and asking questions. Wait for the right moment, and then let it rip.

# Give It Up

Wilma felt as starched and pressed as her tasteful navy blue dress. She was attending a brunch given by her lovely Aunt Beryl, a woman given to extreme formality. Wilma was crazy about her old-school auntie, but she did dread these stiff, rigid social gatherings her aunt seemed to love so much. The guests were always so careful, watching their step to make sure they didn't say or do the wrong thing. And while you were busy minding your p's and q's, you never knew when you'd be "lovingly" assaulted by Aunt Beryl's randy pug, Bobo. Beryl's gatherings always struck Wilma as a sort of obstacle course of etiquette and wild doggy lust.

Out of the corner of her eye, Wilma saw some poor guy try to maintain his dignity while attempting to surreptitiously shake Bobo off his leg. Wilma sighed deeply, knowing this game well herself. Of course, no one ever mentioned Bobo's behavior to Auntie Beryl. It would be like pouring sewage into a Ming vase to sully her kindly, dignified aunt's ear with such a thing. Whenever Beryl saw Bobo mauling some poor victim, she would either avert her eyes with a small, dry cough or call to her "lovely darling" to stop "scratching his fleas" that way. As good a hostess as Aunt Beryl tried to be, she was, and always would be, willfully blind to her precious pug's passion.

Joining her boyfriend, who was talking to a small group of younger folks, Wilma met Sally, the fiancée of one of Beryl's young protégés. This was Sally's first time at a Beryl brunch, and she was talking about her impressions. "This house is so beautiful! And the food is elegant. Wonderful party, really. But what is up with that dog?" She laughed and looked at the group for recognition. Everyone looked down and shuffled their feet or smiled tightly and said nothing. "Oh man," thought Wilma. "We're leaving her hanging." Sally tried again with, "I mean, is there anyone here that dog hasn't tried to hump? On the first date, even!" Sally didn't seem to know that talking about Bobo was simply not done—even though everyone probably wanted to. Now the folks in their little group were embarrassed for her, and she was hanging out there in the wind, waiting for someone to chime in. It was too painful!

Even though Wilma didn't want to hurt her aunt's feelings by impugning her dog's manners, she also couldn't let this poor girl just stand there. "Oh my God, Sally, of course you're right. No one talks about it, I guess because it's not 'polite,' but next time you come to one of Aunt Beryl's gatherings, wear sharp-toed shoes. A swift kick tends to dampen Bobo's ardor." Sally laughed, looking relieved and grateful.

Sometimes you just have to give it up. If your conversation partner seems to really need something from you—your agreement, the willingness to play and be silly, or even some straight-up honesty—it's often best to just be generous enough to give it to them. This generosity is part of being truly open to social interaction, open to receiving and giving back.

Some opportunities for generous communication are

- allowing yourself to be playful when someone teases you gently, even if you feel crabby

- acknowledging a joke with a smile or laugh—even if it's not the funniest thing you've ever heard

- being willing to admit to a similar experience, even if it's embarrassing or controversial

Now, don't go crazy and give it up to everyone, all the time. We don't want you to be anyone's lapdog. But if you see someone struggling or looking for an honest connection in a sincere way, why not be strong and open enough to give 'em some of what they need? It will certainly smooth the conversation—and it may just make you feel like a hero.

# You Do Know!

Julio was finally getting his MBA. He'd always wanted to take that next step in his career, but it'd taken a while to muster up the courage. Now he felt like he was finally in an environment where he could learn all the things he needed to start up his own successful business instead of just working for someone else.

On his papers and exams, he always excelled. Often, though, he felt like he wasn't doing very well in class. Whenever the professor called on him, he felt nervous and sure that he was going to say the wrong thing. Even though he usually managed to articulate an appropriate response, he felt somehow like he came off looking unintelligent. He had a sense that something was wrong about his approach, but he couldn't put his finger on it.

One day his professor interrupted his answer and moved on to another student, even though Julio felt prepared to respond to the question. He knew that his instructor respected his work—she'd said as much in her written comments about his projects. So why had she cut him off?

After class, he went to lunch with his classmates Jackson and Renée. He decided to run the situation by them and see what they thought. Jackson, who was in that particular class with Julio, was well aware of the problem. "No, I don't think it's all in your head. I see it, too. And I think I know what the problem might be. But I feel weird saying it."

"Really? No, please, I'd rather you tell me if it's something I'm doing," Julio said, in complete honesty, even though he was nervous to hear what he might be doing wrong.

"Well, just about every time you talk in class, you start out by saying, 'I don't know, but . . .' And there's something about it, even though I know you know what you're talking about, that makes it seem like you don't. And somehow, even for me, it makes it hard to really hear what you say after that."

Renée, while not in that particular class, had noticed this in Julio as well. "Yeah, I think Jackson is right. I have to admit that I've noticed that, too. But I didn't feel like it was my place to say anything."

Julio felt embarrassed, but he was also grateful to his friends. He'd worked hard to get to where he was in life, and he knew that in business, image and self-presentation meant a lot. It took him a while to break the habit, but eventually he managed to never say "I don't know," unless he really didn't know.

The words you speak as fillers may seem inconsequential, but actually they have a lot of impact on how your audience responds to you. Cutting out or limiting filler phrases like "I don't know," "I guess," or "What do I know?" can help others—and even yourself—see you as more competent and intelligent.

If you really and truly don't know the answer to something, however, you're usually better off not trying to fake it. In most situations it's okay to say, "That's an interesting question. I've never thought about that. What do you think?" or "Honestly, I have no idea." Being able to admit to not knowing—when you actually don't know—makes you appear more confident and assured than trying to pretend you know it all.

# Walk My Way

Sometimes you have to hold firm to get what you want, even if the situation seems hopeless. The art of tactful persuasion can come in handy in these moments.

Jeanette found this to be the case one evening when she went to hear her favorite artist give a free lecture at the local museum. Even though she got there two hours early, all of the tickets had been given out. Many people were being turned away, and she stood there watching them leave. She knew that the British artist didn't come to the United States very often, and that this would be one of her few opportunities to hear the woman speak. "I've always felt that if there's someone or something you need to see, there's got to be a way to make it work. This was a free lecture, after all, and I knew there had to be a way to get inside."

Jeanette went up to the ticket office, smiling her most open and friendly smile. "I went up to the ticket agent and asked her if she knew where the waiting list was. Of course, she said they didn't have one, so I just said, 'Okay, well, I'm going to wait off to the side here, just on the off chance that one or two ticket holders don't show up.'"

Though the ticket agent discouraged Jeanette, reminding her that the event was completely sold out, Jeanette assured her that she didn't mind waiting and thanked the woman for allowing her to do so (even though the agent hadn't actually said as much).

For the next two hours, Jeanette sat on the sidelines, waiting patiently while the audience began to line up outside the door. There were hundreds of people gathering, but she didn't let it faze her. She just kept reading her book and occasionally glancing up to smile casually at the ticket agent.

Once the crowd had finished filing into the auditorium, Jeanette went up to the person at the door and said with polite friendliness, "Hi, I was wondering if by any chance there's a spare seat or a place in the back corner where I could stand." The usher talked to the ticket agent, who told him that Jeanette had been waiting patiently for hours and asked if he could look for a seat for Jeanette. Sure enough, a few people hadn't shown up, and Jeanette scored a spare seat in the fourth row. "It was too bad, because actually there were a half dozen or so seats that ended up being empty. All of those other people who were told it was sold-out just left, but luckily I was able to get myself a seat. It was well worth being persistent!"

The trick to persuading others is to be friendly and not seem at all pushy. Here are some tips to help you get what you want in a respectful way:

- **Always commiserate** ("I understand your hands are tied right now, but would it be okay if I just waited on the off chance that something should change? I understand there may not be any way for you to help me, but I'm willing to take that chance").

- **Don't be too pushy.** If people feel bullied or mistreated, they're not going to want to help you. Never raise your voice or blame the other person if you're trying to persuade them to see things your way.

- **Stand firm.** If you really want something and you're willing to make a sacrifice or be inconvenienced for it, people are generally impressed.

- **Put words in the person's mouth.** Thank them for understanding your predicament, even if they haven't said that they do. Often if you expect people to cooperate and behave accordingly, they'll go along without thinking too much about it.

# No Laughing Matter

Are there times when you just can't keep your mouth shut? More specifically, do you find yourself peppering your conversations with the constant rat-a-tat-tat of nervous laughter? Many of us do. When you're nervous, you may wish you could simply duct-tape your mouth closed so your nervous giggles can't escape. Sheila certainly did.

Sheila was positively freaked. She had finally found herself at the dreaded meet-and-greet party that her law firm gave each spring. As a new employee, this would be the first time she'd be meeting some of the partners, and the scuttlebutt was that they were a stodgy bunch. Every time she thought of engaging one of them, a sharp thrill of panic coursed through her chest. She was as jumpy as a cat.

She gripped her wineglass like a life preserver and ventured forth into the room. Suddenly Sheila felt a small tap on her shoulder. She turned around and came face-to-face with the woman she recognized as the head of the firm. Through her wine- and nerve-induced stupor, Sheila heard the woman known as the Iron Lady introduce herself and inquire how Sheila was liking her time at the firm. "Oh, I love it, Ms. Rogers!" enthused Sheila. "The people are so great—except for the clients, of course!" She felt a loud, braying laugh explode out of her mouth. When Ms. Rogers reminded her gently that the clients were, after all, their bread and butter, Sheila began giggling uncontrollably, nodding and saying, "Yes, oh, of course, sure" as she dissolved into a puddle of mirthful mortification. As Ms. Rogers excused herself, Sheila found that she was *still* giggling—this time so she wouldn't cry.

So many of us have had the experience of being in a nerve-racking social situation and being seemingly unable to stop giggling. Anything we or anyone else says evokes sheer hysteria on our part, while we're thinking to ourselves, "What's happening? That wasn't even a joke! Argh!"

Well, you can give yourself a break. Nervous laughter is something most of us do to fill up the space in a conversation. We laugh as a way to say "I agree," "I'm interested and participating," and "I'm a likable person." It's perfectly okay to use laughter to indicate these things sometimes, but you probably know when you use it too much. If you've ever found yourself sitting at home after a party wondering "What on earth was so funny?" you might want to try the tips below:

- Nervous laughter is first and foremost about, well, nerves. So it makes sense to take some time to calm down before a particularly nervous-making social interaction. Take a moment at home or in your car to breathe deeply, filling your whole belly with air, then letting it out with a whoosh. Remind yourself that even if the interaction goes badly, it's not the end of the world—you will live to chat another day.

- When you feel that wild laughter bubbling up, breathe instead. Take a deep breath as you listen to the other person. This will help you chill and will dampen some of those giggles.

- Try not to be afraid of quiet. In all conversations, especially between new acquaintances, there will be pauses in the conversation. When silence descends, remind yourself that it's fine and natural, and it doesn't mean that the conversation is sinking. You don't need to fill every pause.

- Instead of using laughter to indicate that you're agreeable, interested, and appealing, do it with good eye contact, by listening to what your partner says, and by offering a smile and a nod at the appropriate time. These cues will do fine in getting your message across.

# That's the Way I Like It

Do you find yourself always asking questions, but never really saying what you want? Or do you find yourself telling people what you want, unwilling to budge on the matter? Neither is the ideal way to approach casual social encounters. You want to impress upon people that you are flexible, but that you have a mind of your own and a willingness to express your own needs and desires. How well you strike this balance has a huge impact on the first (or second or third) impression you make on someone.

John was the kind of guy who always wanted to accommodate. He often traveled for his job, visiting other branches of his company all over the world and helping them set up their systems. He met a lot of new people all of the time, and he enjoyed getting to know all about them for the short time he was in town. Often he'd ask one or two of his colleagues to have lunch or dinner, or to spend the day exploring their city with him. He was confident about asking them to join him, but then came the dreaded question: Where do you want to go?

Even though it was John who was new to town, and people generally wanted to do whatever he wanted, it killed him to make a decision. He just kept saying, "Whatever you think." Invariably, they'd make a few suggestions about restaurants and such, offering to let him make the final decision. But he could never decide, because he felt that doing so would be rude. Though he went to more than his fair share of events and eateries that he knew from the start he wouldn't really enjoy, he never said a word or suggested they do something else. He couldn't just say what he wanted.

Lawrence, on the other hand, always felt he had to make the final decision. Whenever he went out on dates, he had to plan everything. He felt that it showed his confidence and strength to plan the entire evening, even making menu suggestions for his date. Because he didn't allow them to give input, he sometimes ended up taking a vegetarian to a steak house, or taking a woman to eat a type of cuisine she already knew she didn't enjoy. Needless to say, he didn't get a whole lot of second dates.

The trick to effective communication about these little things is to make a statement that is clear but not rigid:

- If someone asks you what you want, and you have some idea, then tell them, "Well, I've heard that new Mexican restaurant is really good, but I'm not wedded to that if you have other ideas."

- If you have no idea what you want, you might try "I'm not really sure. But I'd welcome your suggestions, and I'd be happy to give my input."

- If you feel really strongly, try "Well, I've had a hankering for Thai food for weeks. That would be my first choice, though obviously we could do something else if that doesn't sound good to you."

The trick to expressing your desires with people you're just getting to know is being clear and balancing how often you make statements with how often you ask questions. If you just "tell it like it is," people won't feel like there's space for their needs and opinions. If you always hem and haw, and never assert any desires or beliefs of your own, they may find it hard to get to know you. So say what you mean and mean what you say, and give them the space to do the same. That way everyone has a better chance of getting what they want from the situation.

# You've Got a Little Something...

Okay, we've all been there. You're talking to an acquaintance, and you suddenly notice that they have something big and green stuck in their teeth, and it's not going anywhere on its own. *Quel horreur!* Well, maybe it's not the end of the world, but involuntary faux pas like the spinach in the teeth, debris in the nose, or (gasp!) the audible fart can sure distract you from a conversation. What's an innocent bystander to do?

Carrie was really eager to see her new friend, Jennifer. They had met at their women's film group and were just starting to get to know each other. Sitting on the floor with the other film-group gals, she looked up happily when Jennifer came in.

After she'd said hi to everyone and grabbed a plate of snacks, Jennifer came over and sat beside Carrie. But as she smiled hello, Carrie's heart gave a little jump. Jennifer had a big ol' seed or something stuck between her two front teeth. Yow! It looked like a big hole in her mouth. Why hadn't anyone told her about it?

Carrie had a pretty firm feeling about situations like this. She would hate to go through a whole party or even a whole conversation with one person, only to find out later that she'd been flashing remnants of her lunch the whole time. So, because she'd want Carrie to do the same for her, she knew she had to give her the heads up.

Before Jennifer could finish her story, Carrie touched her arm gently and subtly gestured to her own front teeth. "Sorry, but you've got a little . . ." Jennifer's eyes widened a bit and she said "Oh!" as her hand went to her mouth. Carrie quickly took up the conversation, both to show Jennifer that it was no big deal to have something hanging out of her mouth and to give Jen time to remove it. After Jennifer had managed to dig the seed out, she thanked Carrie quietly, and they were able to get on with their conversation.

The key to acknowledging your conversational partner's physical slips or imperfections is subtlety and tact. You may be tempted to totally ignore the problem because you're afraid that mentioning it might embarrass them. But, you must admit, that marred grin can be a real distraction. And wouldn't you want them to tell you? So do it with kindness and discretion. Here are some tips:

- Try not to tell them in front of others. It's best to tell the person one-on-one, but if you're in a group situation, sign language can help. Giving them the eye across the group and subtly pointing at your teeth can send the message discreetly. Even though these things happen to all of us, some folks are more easily embarrassed than others, so it's best to be discreet.

- Keep the conversation going. This will let them know that everything's okay, that you don't feel embarrassed or ashamed of them. Also, your prattling on will provide them cover to do the necessary maintenance.

- Nose debris, eye crud, and earwax are trickier. We advise that you broach these subjects only with those you feel closer to, as they can inspire even more embarrassment.

- Finally, the audible fart. Ah, a special case it is! Ordinarily, farts are the territory of only close friends (or, perhaps, frat brothers). But if you can *hear* the fart, and the other person *knows* you heard it, it becomes very hard to ignore. In this case, the best move is to say "Oops!" signifying that, yes, you heard it, and no, it's not a big deal—because we all do it. (Admit it, now!) Then immediately move the conversation along as though nothing had happened. Voilà!

# Between the Lines

While honesty and saying it like it is might be the conversational ideal, you can't always rely on a new friend or someone you've just met to be utterly direct with you. After all, you haven't had much time to build up trust, and there may be some things that they'd rather not spill right away. You've got to keep your eyes and ears open for the subtle ways they may be saying "Back off."

Walking around the lake, Jenny was really glad to be there with Mark. It was the first time they'd been able to hang out after meeting a few weeks ago at a party, and Jenny was champing at the bit to get to know this tall, dark mystery.

They were having a great time, laughing at the weird folks one inevitably meets at the lake and watching the ducks dive. When Mark asked her what she was doing for the upcoming Thanksgiving holiday, Jenny went into her standard rant about her family. "Oh man, I'm going back to Idaho to have Thanksgiving with my dad this year. I always have to choose between Mom and Dad, even though they live, like, three blocks from each other. But, believe me, I would rather not even try to have some kind of fake happy gathering, forcing them to eat together. They just cannot stand each other since the divorce—even though it happened twelve years ago. So, I've gotta choose between my dad's dried-out turkey and my mom's irritating fussing. I usually just switch off year to year. But enough about me," Jenny smiled. "What are you doing for Turkey Day?" Mark looked away and replied, "Oh, I'm spending it with family, too." Blithely, Jenny charged ahead. "So, you're having it with your mom and dad? Or are they divorced, too? I swear, I don't know anyone whose parents are still together."

Mark replied with a little "Hmm," looking toward the lake and kind of turning away from her. "Wait a minute," thought Jenny. "Why is he acting so weird all of a sudden?" She took another look at Mark's sad expression, his hunched shoulders, and stopped short. "Yikes. He totally doesn't want to talk about this. There's something going on with his family that's hurting him, and I need to lay right off." She quickly changed the subject and breathed a sigh of relief that she'd caught on before backing poor Mark right up against the wall.

Sometimes communication isn't just about what's said, but also about what's not. You may skip happily into a subject you think is perfectly benign, only to find yourself, foot in mouth, trampling someone's feelings. You need to listen between the lines, hearing what the person is omitting and watching their behavior. Here are some things to watch for:

- Does the person you're talking to suddenly seem very quiet? Are they clamming up on you?

- Is their body language unresponsive? Are they averting their eyes, turning away slightly, and looking at the ground? Or maybe you can see a blush creeping up on their cheeks.

These are telltale signs that you're walking on shaky ground. The thing to do is retreat, subtly but immediately, or risk tasting shoe leather—or having your conversation partner go on the attack.

Keep in mind that you need to be aware of who you're talking to, what they're saying, and how they're saying it. And always, *always* bear in mind that you don't yet know where they're coming from. You really have no idea what their experiences or beliefs are—and assuming you do will definitely get you into trouble. So tread lightly and pay attention. You'll be glad you did.

# Whatever!

No matter how good you get at making small talk, you'll always run into the limitations of others. And while it can be tempting to take their bumbling mistakes personally, doing so can make the situation worse for you and even more painful for them.

Sarah had always been the shy, quiet type. Large gatherings of strangers were about as fun as having all of her teeth pulled without the help of drugs. When she was younger, she basked in the idea of working with animals—they never made her feel awkward, they always liked her, and the conversation was blissfully one-sided. But her job as a veterinarian made it necessary for her to interact with strangers every day, often telling them hard things about their beloved pets. It had forced her to get better at making small talk, and, while she didn't relish that part of her job, she had gotten pretty good at it.

When Sarah went out of town to her boyfriend's cousin's wedding, though, she was unprepared for just how bad his family's communication skills were. She was nervous about meeting them for the first time, and she wanted them to like her. Unfortunately, when she and Mike arrived at the wedding site, her encounter with Mike's family went even worse than she'd anticipated. After spending a mere five minutes getting to know her, Mike's mother avoided her for the rest of the day. His father bombarded her with stories about his old Navy days and never once asked her any questions about herself. And Mike's younger brother was a lanky software engineer who couldn't make eye contact with her for more than two consecutive seconds.

She felt mortified that his family was disinterested in her at best, and that night at the hotel she broke down and started crying. Mike, who'd been unaware of the building unhappiness Sarah had been feeling in the hubbub of the day's events, was completely shocked to see her crying. When she told him her worst fears—that his family couldn't stand her and that they'd never accept her—he realized she'd taken their lack of social skills as a sign that they disliked her. "My dad tells *everyone* those stories," he reassured her. "If he hadn't, then I'd have been worried. And my mom is crazy at weddings. She's terrified something will go wrong on their special day, so she's completely distracted. And my brother is just a freak. I love him and all, but he's not exactly Mr. Smooth. Even I find him hard to talk to sometimes, especially at parties."

When Sarah heard him say that, she remembered how awkward she used to be at social gatherings. While her job had improved her communication skills, Mike's brother's field was notorious for doing the opposite. She realized she'd assumed that Mike's family didn't like her, when really it was too soon to jump to any such conclusions.

When you're getting to know people, especially in your first few conversations, you need to remember that most people have a hard time making good small talk. They may be worried you don't like them, they may be preoccupied with things in their lives you have no clue about, or they may just be unpleasant people. Don't jump to any conclusions. If they don't ask you questions, try inserting a story or two about yourself and see if they have the presence of mind to take the bait. If they bail out of the conversation early, don't blame it on yourself. Try a variety of different approaches, and if none of them work, don't hesitate to bail out and move on to the next person—or go home and indulge in a video and a carton of double-chocolate ice cream. You deserve it for all of your efforts!

# Thanks for Sharing

Ensconced on her trusty park bench, Natalie was happily tossing crumbs to the pigeons when an older woman sat down beside her and opened her bag of old bread. "Well, it's nice to be back out in the park after such a hard winter," said the woman as she smiled over at Natalie. "Oh yeah, I love coming here. I worry about my birds when it's too cold to come and feed them." Natalie continued happily feeding her charges. "Oh my," said the lady. "I haven't had a spare moment to worry about the birds, seeing as I've had so many other things to worry about." Sensing that the woman was heading into dangerous territory, Natalie kept quiet. "Let me tell you, when you have a nephew in the hospital, you don't have time to be worrying about birds, oh no." Then, just as if Natalie had responded, "In the hospital? Please tell me more," the old lady proceeded to do just that—in detail.

"Oh my yes, he was in a terrible car wreck, hit head-on, don't you know, and he was just broken. Right leg crushed, bones sticking out here and there. Same thing with the right arm—hanging by a thread, swinging off the stretcher. And the internal injuries! Lord, one of his kidneys was just pulp. They had to pump so much blood into him that they were calling him the Sponge."

Feeling distinctly ill after this delightful tale, Natalie started to wonder whether she'd be tossing her cookies instead of bread crumbs. Did she want to hear any more? No. Did she know how to get out of this without being horribly mean to this poor old lady? Again, no. What should she do?

The way we see it, when you're in a thanks-for-sharing situation, you have five options:

- **Be direct.** This is the conversational ideal: being open and honest, saying something like, "You know, I have a hard time hearing stories about hospitals. I wonder if we could change the subject." Unfortunately, an overdisclosure situation is usually so weird, it can be very difficult to deal openly with the offender.

- **Find your safe place.** This is what many of us do—simply cope until the blabbermouth stops or goes away. Float away to your imaginary safe place: in nature, at your favorite shop, or to a space where you can think about what you'll be doing that night. This is a passive strategy where you mentally escape. This is a good one to use with folks you must not offend (in-laws, bosses), but it can lead to resentment if you lean on it too often.

- **Change the subject.** This is a good bet, if done well. Moving the conversation to a safer (or at least more appetizing) subject will get you out of the situation and prevent you from feeling like a doormat.

- **Leave.** Find a way to make a hasty retreat. Natalie could dump her breadcrumbs and use that as an excuse ("Oh look—all done. Bye!"). Other useful outs are the bathroom, a previous engagement, or getting food.

- **Say it like it is.** This is only for people you think would realize their error. Simply say in a jovial, smiling way, "Whoa! That's a little too much info for me." Again, this works best with folks usually connected to reality who may have just had a temporary slip.

As we all know, getting caught with an overdiscloser is usually a sticky (and tedious) situation. Remember, you have the right to decide what you want—and don't want—to listen to.

# Get Outta There!

It's happened to all of us: there you are, trying to mingle and have a good time at a party where you hardly know anyone, and then you meet someone who decides they're going to be your new best friend. They're nervous, awkward, and a little shy, and you do your best to make them feel at home and be friendly. But then they want to talk your ear off for the rest of the night, and you want to move on and talk to someone new. How can you get out of a conversation gracefully?

That always happened to Rebecca. She was attractive, easy to chat with, and friendly to everyone. She never minded talking to anyone, but sometimes people got the wrong idea. In particular, men often mistook her friendliness for flirting, and once a guy thought she was interested, he wouldn't want to let her out of his sight for the rest of the evening. She didn't want to be mean, but often she just wasn't interested. And even when she was, she felt that it was impolite to talk to just one person in a room filled with people.

At a party it's generally better form to keep moving from one conversation to another. Working the room is more polite than sitting in the corner with one other person, nervously gazing at the others as if they're posing a threat to your personal happiness and to world peace. So whether you're inclined to hide, or you run across a conversation partner who wants to pull you into their private conversation for two, you'll want to try to break away after a while and gab with other folks.

There are several ways to do this without being unfriendly or rude:

- **The straightforward approach.** After twenty or thirty minutes of talking with the same person, if you want to move on, just say, "Boy, it's been great getting to know you, but we shouldn't neglect everyone else. I'm going to go chat with my friend for a while, but maybe I'll see you later in the evening."

- **The cool approach.** If you're not sure you really want to chat later, but the other person isn't terrible either, you can always try something like, "It's been nice talking to you. I'm going to go chat with my friends. Maybe I'll see you later." This approach is for noncommittal types who like to keep their options open.

- **The reassuring approach.** If you're genuinely interested in talking to this person more, but there are a lot of people at the party whom you know and who might be hurt if you didn't make an effort to chat with them (especially if you're the host), try something like, "I'm really enjoying our conversation. I'd love to chat more, but I'm afraid I'm neglecting everyone else. Maybe we could have lunch sometime soon. Let's exchange numbers before we leave tonight."

- **The daredevil approach.** If you really can't stand someone and you need to get away (or the above techniques just haven't worked), you can always say, "Excuse me, I need to use the rest room." After making a pit stop in the bathroom (even if only for show), you can come out and go over to the snacks or join another conversation. It's a little risky, because the other person might come over and say, "Hey, where did you go? I've been looking all over for you!" (In which case, while it may be awkward, you can just say you got caught up with the food or the conversation.) Then again, they may see that you didn't return, take the hint, and find someone else to latch onto for the rest of the night.

# Back on Track

Aha! Gloria spied Georgia from across the room. Georgia was flitting from one conversation to another in her typical social whirlwind. She was what some in the good ol' days might have called a flibbertigibbet—she just couldn't seem to sit still.

Yet Gloria was determined to bring her to earth for at least a short time because she had to—simply *had* to—find out about Georgia's exquisite older brother, Tom. Gloria had met him briefly at a big group picnic a few weeks ago, and she was dying to grill Georgia on his particulars. Now, if she could only pin this bird.

Making her way through the crowded party, Gloria called out and waved to Georgia. "Stay right there," thought Gloria as she zeroed in. Gotcha!

"Hey there, girl!" she smiled. Then she got right to the point. "You know, I wondered if you could tell me about that gorgeous brother of yours. What's his deal?" Georgia giggled and said at top speed, "Oh, Tom. Girls always think he's so cute. 'Course, he's just my brother, so, ick, you know? I mean, I can only see him as a nine-year-old, farting and picking his nose, I mean, ugh! Speaking of which, did you see that guy over there absolutely going *at* it? I mean, talk about mining for gold!"

Interesting as Gloria found discussions of strangers' hygiene habits, she was on a mission. "Well, what does Tom do for a living? Does he have a girlfriend?" Georgia popped a big piece of cake into her mouth and said through the crumbs, "Girlfriend? Oh my God, you should have seen his last girlfriend. I mean, whoa, she was *so* stuck up, I don't know why he didn't break up with her sooner." Gloria was beginning to feel like a dog worrying a bone, but she knew she must stick to this. "But Georgia, does he have a girlfriend now? I'm really interested to know."

Suddenly, like the sun coming from behind a cloud, Georgia's eyes seemed to focus for the first time. "Oh! You like Tom? *Oh* . . . Well, no, he's free as the wind right now. Actually, he's supposed to be here any minute. Wow, I never would have figured that you'd like my brother." She giggled and started in on a litany of her brother's past girlfriends, but at this point it didn't bug Gloria so much. Though she'd felt kind of like a broken record, she'd gotten the scoop she needed.

What can you do when your conversation partner keeps derailing the topic? Well, it pays to be persistent. If it's important to you to continue on that subject, you need to haul the conversation back in that direction. Here are some strategies to help you with the heavy lifting:

- Try to determine whether the person is derailing because they're flighty and inattentive or because they really don't want to talk about it. If you're dealing with someone who just happens to be flaky or manic in the moment, persist in moving the conversation back on track. If there's something more going on, it's probably best to move on.

- Try bringing their attention to the derailing by using phrases like, "Well, back to what I was saying," or "But back to . . ." Some may call this passive-aggressive, but we call it a refreshing reality check. After all, your partner may not realize that they're having trouble staying on track. Try providing a friendly (and do stay friendly about it) reminder.

- Make it personal by owning what you want to talk about. "Oh yeah, I do really want to hear about your root canal, but I wanted to ask you more about that job opportunity at your office." If they don't take subtle hints, it's time to get direct and let them know what you want.

- Finally, if none of these strategies work, it's time to bail. Find another time to broach the subject or another person to have the conversation with. Sometimes it's best to just move on.

# Blowing Off Blowhards

Self-centered. Self-aggrandizing. Full of it. These are all terms that describe garden-variety narcissists, people so in love with themselves that every conversation or interaction inevitably becomes all about *them*. Bane of good conversations everywhere, these blowhards can sometimes be very charming. A typical narcissist trick is to hook you in with charm and flattery, only to turn the tables and begin sucking all the air out of the conversation. Beware the narcissist!

Sean was the new guy in Christopher's little social group. He had somehow managed to make Christopher's friend Sasha fall for him, so now everyone was getting to know the self-appointed greatness that was Sean. And there would be no relief at this New Year's party.

Christopher had kind of liked Sean at first. He'd seemed really interested in Christopher's coaching job at the local high school. But after a while, he always seemed to turn the conversation into a recounting of his glorious days in high school football. How Sean could make every conversation about himself remained a mystery to Christopher—a mystery he would just as soon leave mysterious.

But it was too late. Sean cornered him by the keg. "Hey, man! *Great* to see you, Coach! How's the team shaping up?" Just as Christopher reluctantly began talking, Sean interrupted him. "Oh man, I remember this time of year when I was quarterback. Jeez, Coach Kelly would work us! And, you know, he'd always come down pretty good on me. But now I know it was because he saw some real promise there. And I really did our team proud, if I do say so myself." "Here we go," thought Christopher, settling in to play Sean's audience once again. Eventually Christopher was able to pawn Sean off on some other poor sucker, but not until he'd gotten the stats on all four years of Sean's high school glory—which he'd heard twice before at other parties.

We've all been there, haven't we? We feel forced to listen to some blowhard go off about how great they are, only to leave the conversation feeling a little bit used. They're out there, and the sad truth is that you just can't win with a narcissist. They won't change, and they really don't see what the problem is. They're *really* great and believe that everyone should know about it. So what can you do? Here are some tips:

- **Try to enjoy it.** Lots of narcissists make it their business to be very entertaining. This way, they can attract a bigger audience. The fringe benefit to those of us who are caught in their clutches is that they can be a lot of fun—up to a point. So, no harm in enjoying the show, as long as you know that you're probably never going to get equal time with this cat.

- **Try a little teasin'.** We can't recommend this as the healthiest strategy, but if you're stuck dealing with a blowhard, you may want to indulge in some gentle ribbing. Don't get mean, but the passive aggression of playfully taking them down a notch may help you cope when you're forced into perpetual audience mode. Just don't tell your therapist about it.

- **Get outta there.** The last word on narcissists is that you don't want to be with them. Even if they can be fun, eventually we all tire of being supporting players in someone else's show. So if you spot a narcissist, we recommend that you do your darndest to have as little to do with them as you can. If you're talking to someone who can only relate to how things affect them, that's your cue to clear out and stay clear.

Now, we can all stray into narcissist territory once in a while, occasionally talking a wee bit too much about our thing. That's natural. The folks you want to avoid are those for whom this is a regular gig. Trust us, you don't want to attend that show.

# Mum's the Word

What you don't say is sometimes just as important as what you do say. While it can be tempting at times to ramble on and make your point repeatedly, using silence as a conversation strategy can be a powerful tool.

Emily felt like she had the word "pushover" emblazoned across her forehead. It seemed like strangers could tell in a matter of seconds that they could win in any disagreement they had with her. They cut in front of her in lines, cheated her out of her correct change, and generally walked all over her. She wanted to be nice, and she hated the idea of ever yelling at someone, but she was sick of being a doormat.

Things came to a head one day when her home phone line went down. She called the phone company, and they told her that she'd have to be home from eight to five the next day. Even though she didn't have much sick time left, she had no choice but to stay home and waste her day watching soap operas and waiting for the repair person to arrive.

Except that they didn't. Five o'clock came and went, and she'd been at home all day for nothing. Even being the softy she was, Emily felt her blood going at a mild simmer. She couldn't miss the next day at work, and she needed to get her phone working.

When she called the company, they told her that someone should have been there. "Are you sure you were there *all* day?" the woman asked accusingly.

"Yes, I'm positive. I didn't leave my apartment once all day long. I haven't even been outside yet today, even though it's beautiful outside," Emily said, trying to keep her voice calm and steady.

"Okay, well, you're just going to have to be there all day tomorrow. And this time you need to make sure you don't go anywhere."

That was Emily's that's-it moment. She wasn't going to be pushed around this time. "Look, I had to miss work all day today for nothing. And I was here all day today. I can go in a few hours late and stay late, but I can't just sit here all day again. I need to do my job. You're going to need to send someone out at eight A.M. so that I can let them in and then go to work."

"I can't do that ma'am."

Emily was silent.

"Ma'am?"

"I'm here," was all Emily would say.

After a few rounds of this, the woman finally sighed. "Okay, I'll see what I can do. We'll get someone out there first thing in the morning."

As Emily learned, sometimes it's most effective to say what you need to say and then stop saying anything. Often, otherwise difficult people will be intimidated by your silence. And many others will realize that you're a force to be reckoned with, and they may decide that it's easier to give you what you want than to fight with a silent front.

When using this tactic, it's important to first calmly state your grievance and make it clear how you would like it to be resolved. You may need to repeat yourself once, but doing so more than once simply weakens your stance. If someone asks for clarification, of course you want to give it to them. But if they just want to jerk your chain, and you're sure that you're justified in holding firm, allow yourself to bask in your own silence and let them squirm a bit.

# Tears without Fears

Whenever she gets sick, Becca becomes a fully operational tear factory. Sappy commercials, stern looks, or an overly tight jar lid can take her from normal to weepy in a matter of seconds. Her job as a pediatrician means she's exposed to every cold and flu that goes around. While she's as healthy as a rhino, she inevitably gets sick. Pair that with her long hours with screaming kids, and you've got a recipe for a crying jag that just won't quit.

When the stakes are high, Becca's able to put on her professional persona and get to work. But somehow that just doesn't work with the little things, when she's let down her guard. Like the time the hospital cafeteria worker wouldn't let Becca grab something hot to eat before the kitchen closed for the evening.

"I just couldn't handle another cold bagel for dinner. I needed something that was going to help me get through the last three hours of my shift, but she wanted to go home. I could see that they'd just started putting the hot food away, though, and I couldn't understand why she wouldn't help me out. And right there, in the middle of my indignant protests, I started to cry in front of the entire cafeteria staff. It was mortifying!"

If you're in a situation where you start crying and it feels inappropriate or overwhelming, don't give up trying to get your view across. Crying is a natural stress release, and it doesn't have to end a conversation or ruin your credibility if you maintain your dignity. Here are some things you might want to do to help keep your footing if you've started to cry:

- **Don't apologize for the tears.** You haven't done anything wrong, and saying you're sorry implies that you have.

- **Acknowledge that you're upset.** Becca's tears actually helped her make her case. She just said, "As you can see, I'm upset because I'm sick and very tired, and I really need something hot to eat." If, in all fairness, you know you're being unreasonable and you want to defuse the situation, you can always try saying, "Wow! I'm feeling emotional today. What side of the bed did I get up on?"

- **Give yourself space to cry.** If you need a minute to compose yourself, just say, "Nature calls!" and make confident strides toward the nearest bathroom.

In the end, the cafeteria workers made Becca a dinner plate, and today she is very matter-of-fact about the experience: "I cried because I was frustrated. That doesn't mean I'm not a smart, strong doctor who is good at my job, it just means that those frickin' scientists need to work a little harder on finding the cure for the common cold!"

Crying in front of someone you don't know very well can be awkward and humiliating if you react to it as such. But if you treat it openly (or humorously, if the situation calls for it), then you can go ahead and let the good tears roll.

# Flip Tip

If you're in a conversation with someone who is crying (or who always seems to cry), you can be compassionate, offer them a tissue, or give them the chance to take a break from the conversation. That said, there's no need to back off from your viewpoint or your goal in the conversation. As long as you're being respectful and not resorting to name-calling or other kinds of derision, you have every right to hold firm.

# I Don't Think So

Do you love conflict? Probably not—most of us avoid it like the plague. And many of us assume that by contradicting another person, we're necessarily starting a conflict. But this doesn't have to be so. Whether you're in the friendliest or most formal social situation, you certainly have a right to state your views, even if they contradict someone else's. And if you do it with firmness and respect, you'll be able to make your point without making anyone mad.

"Oh boy, here she comes," thought Ted as he spied Christine bearing down on him. Ted liked to think of himself as a pretty tolerant person, but Christine was beyond the pale. After having met Ted only a few times, she seemed to think that they were best friends. What's worse, she was under the impression that she knew—really *knew*—Ted's mind. She seemed to love putting forth opinions for him in every social situation they'd been in together. And she was consistently, maddeningly wrong.

"Oh hey, Ted! This is my friend Cathy," Christine gestured toward the good-looking bespectacled woman standing next to her. "I'm so surprised to see you here, Teddy. I know you can't stand getting your hair wet, and it sure is coming down." "Here we go," thought Ted. He had no idea where she'd gotten this false factoid, but he just nodded and smiled in response, letting it slide. The last thing he wanted was to get into an argument with her right in front of the increasingly appealing Cathy.

They continued to talk, with Ted trying to engage Cathy and Christine trying to help by letting Cathy know all about the "real" Ted. She ventured incorrect opinions for him about sports (didn't like 'em), politics (totally not interested), and women (liked 'em blond). But she crossed the line with this last one.

Ted took a breath, reminded himself that Christine probably meant well, and said, "Actually, Christine, that's not true. I don't have any type when it comes to women I find attractive." Looking at the amused (and raven-haired) Cathy, Ted finished with, "In fact, my last two girlfriends were brunette."

Christine stopped (finally!), looking confused. Ted had never really contradicted her before, and it obviously threw her. "Oh, I didn't know that. Hmm . . . um . . . well, you know, I'm gonna get a drink." She wandered off, deflated, leaving Ted to find out more about Cathy.

As you can see, when Ted finally stood up for his opinion, he stopped feeling railroaded and got what he wanted in the conversation. You can too by considering these tips for contradicting courteously:

- Remember that you have the perfect right to voice your opinion, even if it contradicts someone else's.

- Just because you have the right doesn't mean you should feel compelled to contradict in all cases. Choose your occasions well, considering whom you're talking to, how important the issue is to you, and how you should phrase your contradiction to best be heard. Also, if it's an issue that you feel very emotional about, consider whether the situation is appropriate and whether you can voice your opinion in a calm, fair way. If not, forego the opportunity.

- Contradict with respect. You don't have to make the other person seem bad or wrong—just offer your view.

- Remember to phrase your contradiction as your view, opinion, or experience. Claiming an absolute truth ("That record was hack-spewed swill," instead of "I didn't think it was his best work") is sure to get you into trouble, because it doesn't respect the other person's right to an opinion.

# Mind Your Own Beeswax!

While it's great to have a conversation with someone who seems engaged and genuinely interested in getting to know more about you, sometimes you might be asked questions that you don't feel comfortable answering. Maybe you're in a public setting and the topic is a private one that's best saved for one-on-one conversations. Or maybe you just don't know the person well enough to disclose personal information. So how do you politely tell them to mind their own business?

This happens to Zadie all of the time. She works for the government, and much of her work is classified. "It drives me crazy, because 'What do you do?' is one of the most common small-talk questions of all time. Sometimes people will let me get away with saying I work for the government, but usually they ask more specific questions about my job."

Zadie realizes that most of the time people are just asking well-intentioned questions in an effort to express interest in her. "It's tough. Sometimes I'll try to respond a bit and say I work for the CIA, but inevitably that raises more and more questions. I'll tell them it's classified, and often that either provokes them to try and pry further or makes them back off because they're afraid I'm some kind of dangerous spy."

While not all of us have a top secret job to protect, most of us do have some off-limits subjects that we don't want to discuss with people we don't know well. Most people feel some level of discomfort discussing their personal finances, their most impassioned political and religious views, or their sex lives with people they've just met. And, as individuals, many of us have topics that are more complicated or distressing for us than they would normally be for someone else.

If you run into one of these danger zones with someone you don't have any interest in getting to know better, first try to change the subject. If they don't let it go, be polite but firm: "I appreciate your interest, but I'd be more comfortable talking about something else."

But what if you're talking to someone you'd really like to get to know better? At parties, Zadie often found that she'd be talking to women that she was attracted to, only to have the dreaded work conversation come up. "Who wants to date someone who can't talk about her job? I mean, a lot of people wouldn't want to deal with that, and it's a pretty big thing to have to confront someone with before you've even gone out on your first date! I always get flustered."

In this case, when you'd like to let the person know that you're changing the subject, but you still really want to talk with them, there are several things you can try:

- **Answer the question briefly and then reciprocate.** In Zadie's case it can work to say, "I work for the government, but I'm not at liberty to talk about it. But I'd love to hear about what you do."

- **Answer and then change the subject:** "I work for the government, but I really love going to the movies. What have you seen recently?"

- **Postpone the conversation:** "That seems like a conversation for another time and place. But I'd love to hear about that vacation you mentioned earlier."

# To the Not-So-Bitter End

In most conversations, trying to win is a losing proposition. Sure, there are times when you really need to push your way through, fight for what you believe in, and stick up for yourself or others. But most of the time when you're making small talk, you need to try to see the other person's point of view and, if necessary, amicably agree to disagree.

Mahlia works for a grassroots environmental organization that lobbies to protect the health and well-being of people and wildlife. She works long hours for low pay, but she loves her coworkers and she believes in the work she does. While she tries not to turn it on too strong, she knows she can be a bit of a judgmental diehard when people don't care enough about the issues she's fighting for every day. Usually she just tries to avoid sensitive topics with people she knows are more conservative than she is, but when her buttons get pushed she's been known to argue with strangers for hours, trying to convince them to see things her way.

"One time, this guy at a party started going off about how ridiculous it was for the government to make the private sector buy a certain amount of products made from recycled materials. Well, I'd been busting my hump for months trying to get that very mandate passed, and I just lost it. I told him that if he liked breathing the air he was breathing, and drinking the water he was drinking, he might want to reconsider his capitalist views and start thinking about what he could do to protect our environment. Needless to say, my tactics weren't all that successful. He and I were both pissed, and by the end of it everyone else just sort of moved away from us, and I was left to fight with him all night. It was a mess!"

When small talk leaves the realm of small subjects and touches on something you value or despise, it can be tempting to launch into a full-fledged battle to the death. But remember, it's a party. Your hosts aren't going to be happy if you fight with other guests, and no one is going to have a good time. Here are some ways to deal with sensitive issues in casual conversations:

- **Don't bring them up.** If you're in mixed company and you're an activist for a controversial issue (or you're just plain opinionated), don't raise the topic yourself. If you know that talking politics or religion or books or cooking makes you crazy whenever people disagree with you, have the good sense not to bring the problem on yourself.

- **Keep it cool.** If someone says something offensive (and you know it's going to happen), don't make things worse by immediately flying off the handle. People say stupid things all the time. Learn to pick your battles. Of course, if your conscience and integrity require that you respond to the bigoted party guest or the loudmouth family member, go right ahead. But try to be tactful, and keep your focus on avoiding a full-blown argument. Saying calmly, "I can't say I agree. Perhaps we should change the subject," is a better way of handling small talk gone bad, as opposed to resorting to name-calling or voice raising.

- **Keep an open mind.** Approaching a conversation as an argument means missing out on the opportunity to at least understand the other side of the story. You don't have to change your mind (or theirs), but being open to the possibility can make the conversation more interesting and less traumatic for all those involved.

# Rock Steady

Tony had just heard that he'd gotten the job of his dreams, a job that he'd been trying to get for weeks now. He was so excited, he felt like he was going to bust. He yanked up his telephone and punched in Brian's number.

And he was off! The moment Brian said hello, Tony was into his story, full speed ahead. He was just so excited about the news that he couldn't talk fast enough. He felt like if he slowed down, he might just explode with all the words that needed to be said.

Meanwhile, on the other end of the line, Brian was just waking up from a nap. He picked up the phone only to find a machine gun going off in his ear. With each rat-a-tat-tat of Tony's voice, Brian wished more fervently that he had let the machine get this one. He did care about Tony finally getting the job, but he felt like he had a woodpecker tied to his head, pecking out his brain.

This often happened between these two friends. Tony couldn't seem to talk fast enough, spewing out information at the speed of light, while Brian was a bit more meandering in his style. They'd known each other for a few years now, and each liked the other's different energy. But sometimes the differences in their conversational rhythm could drive each of them crazy. During this exchange, for instance, Brian was wishing Tony would stop talking his ear off, while Tony was hoping that Brain would wake up. Who's right?

They both are. Like most human interactions, conversation is about compromise. Like our parents taught us when we were little kids, we must remember to share. That means that no one person in the conversation gets to always choose the topic, control how much each person says, or determine the rhythm of the conversation. They have to come to an agreement about these things through give-and-take. So, in the case of Brian and Tony, maybe Tony will stop jawing for a second and notice that Brian sounds like he's still in a nap stupor. Or maybe Brian makes an effort to summon some energy and talk faster. Either way, each person is keyed in and paying attention to where the other is coming from. Then they can come to a compromise, usually unspoken, about how the rhythm will work from there.

Here's the pattern, broken down:

- **Check out your partner's rhythm.** When you start talking to someone, you may not even notice the rhythm of the conversation because it's just smooth—you're matching each other's speed pretty well. But if the person you're engaged with is talking more quickly or slowly than you, take a moment to note this.

- **Decide how you feel about it.** Is their energy infectious, so you don't mind speeding up a bit? Could their leisurely conversational pace be a nice break for you? While you're talking, decide whether or not you want to hop aboard their rhythm.

- **Choose your tack.** You can either attempt to match their speed or go ahead with your own, hoping they'll clue in and adjust to you. Try not to let this get passive-aggressive—"showing" them by slowing down to a snail's pace or revving up to supersonic speed. Presumably, you want to make this exchange a pleasant one. You might even suggest that they try to match your rhythm ("Whoa nelly! Slow down a bit"), though this would have to be done carefully—and probably just with speedy gabbers.

- **Wait until later.** If neither of you can seem to adjust to the same rhythm, try not to take it personally. You may just want to withdraw a bit and save the conversation for another time. Maybe later you'll be rockin' to the same beat.

# Get a Little Closer

When small talk goes well and you're really hitting it off with someone, you may find that you want to ask the person to hang out with you again. Even if it's just someone you want to be friends with, asking someone out can be nerve-racking. Especially if you think the person is really fun and charming, it can be just like when you were dating in school: your heart starts pounding as your mouth tries to form the words, and you hope they don't think, "Ew. Why would I want to hang out with *you?*"

Brenda recently went through a nasty divorce that left her living in a tiny apartment instead of her nice house. Her couple friends all seemed uncomfortable around her, like she had some kind of contagious breakup disease. She was lonely, she missed her life, and she was tired of renting movies by herself every night. She had a few close friends she could talk to, but mostly everyone was busy with their own jobs and kids and partners, and no one had time during the week to have dinner or get together.

One night she went to a restaurant down the street from her house. She was reading *The Great Gatsby,* a book she'd always wanted to get to but never had. At least her breakup was enhancing her brain, she thought to herself on a regular basis. She sat down and ordered dinner, and began reading while she waited for her food.

While she was waiting, another woman sat down at the table next to her and pulled out a book. Brenda glanced up and was surprised to see that the woman was also reading *The Great Gatsby.* Sure, it was a classic. But what were the odds? Brenda felt she had to say something. "How are you enjoying it?" she asked, smiling and holding up her own copy.

The woman laughed with delight. "How funny! I'm enjoying it quite a bit, thanks. And you? What part are you at?"

As they chatted about the book, Brenda found out that she and the woman, Claire, actually had a good deal in common. Before she knew it, her food was arriving, and they were still chatting. While she felt shy, especially since it had been a few years since she'd made a new friend, she decided to take a chance and ask Claire to join her for dinner. Claire agreed with enthusiasm, and they had a lovely dinner together chatting about their favorite books and movies. At the end of the evening, Claire asked Brenda if she'd like to have dinner again sometime, and soon they established a regular Tuesday night dinner date that they both looked forward to each week.

You never know when you're going to meet interesting people. Especially if you're hoping to expand your social circle, you want to stay open to the possibility of making contact with someone new and putting yourself out there by inviting them to spend time with you again in the future. It's true that they might not have the time or space to say yes, and that can feel mortifying in the moment. But inevitably the only way to meet new friends (or sweethearts, for that matter) is to take a chance when the opportunity presents itself.

While it may feel hard, the steps themselves are quite easy. Simply pay the person a compliment. Something like, "You're really fun to talk to," or "I've enjoyed hearing your opinions about local politics. Would you be interested in going to the upcoming debate with me?" Offer your e-mail address or phone number, and suggest a specific activity if one comes to mind. Likely they'll be flattered, and you'll both have the opportunity to take a chance encounter and turn it into something deeper.

# Riff Master

Hey, hey, hey! Hoo, hoo, hoo! You're a lean, mean riff machine. You make witty jokes and slide in clever comments. You're poised on the edge of every conversation, looking for what's being said, what's not being said, and which words sound just plain funny. You build on the conversation, taking twists and turns, and taking on various personas as you go. If you can master the art of riffing and you're in a crowd that values the form, you're sure to be the life of the party every time.

Riffing is one of the ultimate small-talk successes. It's fun and funny. It shows people that you're really listening to them and that you're really engaged. And it lets them know you're not just some boring stuffed shirt or timid wallflower. But if you've never riffed before, how are you ever going to be good at it? You just have to start churning those rusty old wheels. Only practice will get you running smooth.

The whole point of riffing is to have a fast, flowing back-and-forth that has a whip-smart attitude and a healthy dose of humor. When done correctly, it can make a conversation (and an evening) fly by on a high dose of laughter and adrenaline. If you're ready to try it, consider the following:

- **Timing is everything.** Riffing is about chemistry and the moment. You don't riff at funerals. You do riff at parties. You don't walk up to a conversation and launch into riffing. You build up, get the laughter going, and then build to the full riff potential.

- **Be a riffing apprentice.** When someone says something that makes you think of something funny, throw it in there. Experiment with funny tones of voice and speech patterns. Try a deadpan style, or a tongue-in-check I'm-a-know-it-all-and-I-know-it voice. Tease a little, but don't say anything mean.

- **Test the waters.** Not everyone can riff, and not everyone feels comfortable with that style of communication. If you try to riff with someone and they don't take the bait or they seem uncomfortable, then abort. They may misunderstand and think you're making fun of them, and you don't want to hurt anyone's feelings. Be sensitive to your surroundings. Riffing is a high form of chatty-chat, and not everyone is ready.

- **Don't try this on your own.** Remember, it does take two to riff. You might throw in a joke or two or make a clever play on words. But if your conversation partner can't play along, then you end up playing the role of stand-up comedian in your own one-person show. And how boring (and potentially obnoxious) is that?

- **Recycle and reuse.** Bringing up things from past conversations, or from earlier in the same conversation, is a great riffing strategy. People will love how you string earlier jokes together with newer ones. It shows them you're paying attention, and that your brain is big and shiny.

- **Find a couple of good lines or jokes that work,** and sprinkle them in occasionally. For instance, if someone is talking about their recent car repair, they might say, "I hope it just lasts and lasts." If you have previous riffing experience with them, you can throw in a zinger like, "That's what my last date said." Riff, riff, and away.

# Talk Hog

"Uh-huh . . . Right. I think . . . Uh-huh. Well, sure, but . . . Yeah . . . Right . . . Uh-huh," Max rolled her eyes at Erin, twisting the phone cord in her hand while she listened to her mom drone on and on about her new neighbors. "Yep. Mom, I really need to . . . Uh-huh. Well, I hope it gets better. Okay . . . okay. Oh, okay, I'll talk to you later. Bye, Mom."

"Argh!" Max screamed, slamming down the phone.

"What was it this time? The price of vegetables? The problem with kids these days?" Erin knew how Max's mom could be when she got onto one of her favorite subjects.

"No, now her new neighbors are parking their car on the street too close to her driveway. You'd think they were trying to run her down with their car, the way she's reacting. I couldn't get a word in edgewise."

"Did you tell her we wouldn't be going there for Christmas this year?" Erin asked.

"No, but really, she wouldn't have listened if I *had* said something. I think I'll have to call while she's at work and leave her a voice mail message. At least then I'll get to talk!"

Max's mom is notorious for being a talk hog. She never listens, she doesn't take any cues when people are trying to change the subject or end the conversation, and she rarely asks other people about their lives. As a result, Max feels like she has to find ways around her mom, and in the end Max often tries to avoid talking to her.

What do you do if someone you know is a big ol' talk hog? If the person is someone you love, you need to butt in and stake your claim on your rightful half of the conversation. If that doesn't work, then it might be time to address the subject more explicitly: "I really love talking to you, but sometimes I wish you'd ask me more questions and spend more time listening to what I have to say." Being respectful but up-front is the best thing you can do, both for the other person and for yourself.

With acquaintances, especially if they're bombarding you with a one-way debate, you might try: "I hear what you're saying, and now I'd like for you to extend me the courtesy of hearing me out." Whether they're on a roll or they're just plain rude and inconsiderate, some people need to be reminded that a conversation is a dialogue and not a monologue. Don't let a talk hog bully you into sullen silence.

# Flip Tip
Flip Tip

Do you suspect that you might be a talk hog? Perhaps you talk a lot because you're nervous, or because you're terrified of awkward silences, or because you're eager to impress. At parties, do you feel like you get on a roll and end up crushing everyone around you with an endless barrage of jokes or stories? If you fear the worst, muster up your courage and ask a few people who are close to you if they sometimes feel like you talk their ear off. Ask if they feel like they get enough space in the conversation, and try to be open to their feedback.

Some general rules for chronic talk hogs: Make sure to ask the other person questions in every conversation, even something as simple as, "How are things going?" Don't forget to ask follow-up questions about past conversations ("So how did that meeting go, anyway? I know you were nervous about it"), as well as during each conversation ("That sounds interesting. Why did you decide to try skydiving?). These simple steps can help keep you from offending others or causing them to misinterpret your chattiness as disinterest in what they have to say.

# Pump It Up, Take It Down

Nate was renowned for his soft-spokenness. Even among his close friends, he tended to be subdued, but at parties, his speech was positively tortoiselike—slow and hesitant. At best, he played the thoughtful observer of conversations, nodding his head like a bobblehead toy. Usually he ended up alone in the corner, trying to blend in with the houseplants.

At his friend's annual holiday party last year, he found himself camouflaged in a fern, counting the minutes until he could politely make his exit. And then in walked Nicole. She had a laugh that was a freakish hybrid between a donkey and a pig: hee-haw-hee-haw-*snort!* He watched from his cave as she worked the room and chattered with every person she encountered. It wasn't long before she'd worked the entire room, and she narrowed in on him. As she approached, Nate felt his throat clench.

"Hey, there! My name is Nicole. I'm friends with Frank and Jackie. We've known each other for years and years. I used to work with him, and then her, and then I temped for her cousin. I'm practically like family. Or at least the frequently unemployed cousin they never knew they wanted. Hee-hee-hee-*snort!* And who are you?"

"I'm Nate."

"Well, my oh my, Nate! You're quite the talker. Did anyone ever tell you that? Hee-haw!"

Okay, stop. How in the world are someone like Nate and someone like Nicole ever going to have a conversation? At this rate, she's going to race over him and crush him like an unlucky turtle who wandered unknowingly into the middle of the Indy 500. And she's never going to hear a word he says, because she's racing past him like a hare out of hell. The only way for these two—who actually have a lot in common—to connect in any successful way is for Nate to pump it up and for Nicole to take it down.

Matching your speech rhythm and volume with the person you're talking to makes it much easier to talk. Be sensitive to your audience. While you don't need to match them exactly, there's no point in talking over someone for twenty minutes, and it's no fun to be talked over. Adjusting to a similar level is something that the best conversationalists do without thinking—and luckily it's a skill that the rest of us can master with practice.

When you enter into a conversation with someone at that next cocktail party, here are some things to consider:

- **Volume.** If someone has a soft voice, tone your own down so that you don't overwhelm the person and you can hear what they're saying. This doesn't mean you have to whisper. Meet them halfway, give the conversation a whirl, and if they refuse to speak up a bit (or talk at all), then make your way to the next person in the crowd.

- **Speed.** Again, meet in the middle. This shows, even subliminally, that you're making an effort to put the person at ease and get to know them.

- **Topics.** If they're talking about the weather, don't delve into your history with your therapist. If the person is a heavyweight (talking about Nicaraguan politics) and you want to change the subject, go to something of medium weight (recent elections) instead of featherweight (your favorite sitcom).

# Let's Get Physical

You may not think about it a lot, but you're sending messages with each move you make. By how you hold yourself, how you use your eyes, and what you're doing with your arms and legs, you're telling people how you feel about them, yourself, and the situation. Wouldn't it be great to start transmitting the messages you want to send?

Calvin was nervous. He could hardly believe he was sitting at a café with Mary, the woman he'd wanted for months to date. Though their conversation seemed to be going okay, he just didn't feel that Mary was really opening up to him. She seemed reserved, as though she didn't really like him that much. Though Calvin continued making jokes and trying to keep the conversation light, inside he was starting to worry that he was blowing it.

When Mary excused herself to go to the bathroom, Calvin took his first look around the café. He saw people sitting all around him enjoying themselves, relaxed and laughing. There was one couple sitting across the room who seemed to be having a great time. The woman looked positively delighted to be sitting with the guy. "What's he doing that I'm not?" thought Calvin.

Then Calvin took a closer look. For one thing, the guy just seemed relaxed. He was smiling and his shoulders weren't all scrunched up around his ears, the way Calvin's were. He also looked interested. He was leaning forward, nodding at what his date was saying, and looking her in the eye. "Gee, I wouldn't mind talking to him myself," mused Calvin.

Calvin took one look at his own body and realized what might be turning Mary off. He was twisted up like a pretzel, with his arms and legs crossed. He remembered also that he had felt really shy about meeting Mary's gaze or even smiling too much at her—didn't want to scare her off. But it dawned on him that maybe his body language *was* scaring her off.

When Mary returned, Calvin made a conscious effort to open up and connect with her. He uncrossed his limbs, relaxed his shoulders, and started showing Mary he was really listening by nodding and smiling at her stories. He found that as he opened up, he was able to concentrate more on her than on himself, and discovered that he was actually enjoying himself, leaning forward with interest and even giving a few belly laughs. And when Mary laughed at one of his jokes and put her hand briefly over his on the table, he knew she was having fun, too.

Opening up to someone doesn't mean baring your soul (not on the first date, please). It means letting your gestures and posture—your body—be open. This kind of nonverbal affirmation works wonders because it's so honest. The other person can *feel* that you're interested—and you can read their body language to see how they're feeling, too.

Here are some pointers to get your body in shape for conversation:

- **Uncross your arms and legs.** Let your body seem open to the conversation.

- **Lean forward slightly to listen.** Don't get in the person's face—just indicate that you're interested.

- **Make eye contact.** Make sure your eyes move to meet each person's gaze if you're talking to more than one person. As you talk, hold eye contact for two to four seconds, then move on.

- **Use facial expressions.** Who wants to talk to a mask? Use a smile, raised eyebrow, or even a frown to indicate that you're listening and engaged.

It's natural that we all read people's bodies as much as their words, even if we're not aware of it. Make sure your bod's sending the right signals!

# Stop, Look, and Listen

It's always a good idea to check out someone's body language when you're talking to them. After all, they may be sending you important messages that they can't, or won't, say out loud ("I really like you," with a big smile and touch on the shoulder; "I'm very shy," by looking down and crossing their arms). But what about when you find your conversational partner's body language, well, perplexing?

"Oh no, here she comes," thought Jackson as Martha moved toward him in the crowd. Jackson didn't know Martha very well, but he had already categorized her as one of those folks who he referred to as "starey-scary." She had an unfortunate habit of bugging her eyes out and staring fixedly at you while you talked, all the while smiling widely and nodding. Jackson had no idea what she was thinking or why she couldn't seem to pull her peepers off of his face, but it really bothered him. And now it was too late—she'd pinned him.

"Hey, Jackson! I'm so glad I caught you. I really wanted to hear how your new job is going." Martha smiled widely at him, already nodding. Jackson sighed inwardly and started in on his story, but Martha's constant, seemingly unblinking gaze was beginning to unnerve him. He always got this way with folks who didn't say much or whose behavior he couldn't quite peg. He became the talking machine, babbling at an increasingly fast pace until he felt like he was in danger of taking off into the stratosphere. And because he couldn't read Martha by her unchanging—some would say bug-eyed—expression, his nerves made him act like some performing circus monkey.

"Wellyouknow,I'vegotagreatofficewithaviewandIlikeallthenewfolksI'mmeeting."

At this point, Jackson was talking a mile a minute, but as his verbal bullet train shot down the track, he suddenly thought to himself, "Wait a minute. What am I doing? No wonder she does nothing but stare. I haven't asked her a thing about herself! I just get so nervous looking at those big, starey eyes that I can't seem to shut up. I need to take a chill pill."

Jackson put on the brakes (although at this point it seemed as though his mouth had a mind of its own) and took a deep breath. Then he smiled at Martha and asked, "But how are *you* doing? Tell me about the new baby." After that, even though Martha tended to talk haltingly and continued to fix him with her blue-eyed stare, Jackson could relax enough to let her be.

When we're faced with indirect conversational styles—staring, mumbling, hmm-ing—a lot of us react by going into overdrive. Because we're just not sure where our partner is coming from, we freak out and decide that any space in the conversation means death. So we either talk their ears off—or we simply try to get away.

But glory be, there is a solution! Recognize that no matter how indirect or even bizarre someone else's conversational style, your *reaction* to it is up to you. So instead of reacting with nerves or even horror, you can choose to take a breath, stop the nervous chatter, and ask the person a question. This will give them a chance to talk (which your nerves may not otherwise allow) and will reveal what they're actually thinking, so you don't have to make assumptions. After all, you don't know why they're behaving this way—maybe they were raised to always make fierce eye contact or to never, never interrupt.

So the next time you're faced with an indirect conversational style, remember that you don't have to compensate. You can let it be, let *them* be whomever they are. Just try breathing and listening instead of filling the space. You may be surprised what you finally hear.

# Work It

When you're talking with a bunch of people, you can either blend into the scenery or work the crowd and make people feel at ease. Learning how to work group dynamics to your advantage can make you the life of the party, and can come in handy at business meetings and family gatherings.

Maggie had been out of work for eight months. She'd sent out dozens of résumés and chatted with all the people she knew about potential leads, but nothing had materialized. Finally, she broke down and started going to networking events.

At the first few events, she slunk around the darkest corners of the room, nursing her drink and wishing the ground would open up and swallow her whole. She chatted with a few people, but she never had the nerve to give anyone her business card or suggest that they get together. She watched other people do it, but she couldn't find the courage.

Over time, though, desperation and a good deal of boredom forced her to study the behaviors of some of the other people at these events—the people she envied, and, for a brief little while, even hated. She started trying out one new tactic at each event, and over time she started talking to many more people. Here are some of the behaviors she co-opted:

- **Eye contact.** Make it with everyone in the general vicinity. It's good for you, and it makes others like you more.

- **Make sure everyone feels included.** If someone is standing on the outskirts of your conversation, looking for a way to break in, smile at them or wave them into the circle. Nod when everyone is talking. Smile, ask interested questions, and add tidbits about yourself into the conversation.

- **Use welcoming body language.** Don't fold your arms across your chest or stuff your hands in your pockets in these moments, no matter how comfortable it may feel. Don't stand in front of people or edge them out of the circle of conversation. Assuming the position of welcoming others makes you feel more comfortable, and it ingratiates you to others who appreciate feeling included.

- **Put yourself out there.** Go ahead and be the first person to pay someone a compliment, or ask a question that makes you a little vulnerable (say, about something you know nothing about but are interesting in learning). If you're at a party, a networking mixer, or some other event where you're unlikely to run into each other again, offer your phone number to people you meet and suggest a casual get-together. If you're trying to get a job or a date, or you're really wanting to expand your network of friends, try making yourself give your number to at least one person at every event.

- **Go for the gusto.** Walk up to the crowd that contains the person in the room who interests you most, for whatever reason. Sticking with the people who aren't in your field, or who you don't find attractive, or with whom you have nothing in common, isn't going to get you anywhere.

Over time, Maggie absorbed this information and started using it herself. At first, she just made her way into a small circle of people, smiling and nodding. But after a few months of regular practice, she started having coffee with a bunch of people in her field. It led her to a new job that she was relieved to have, and it also left her with a few new friends.

# Wheeler-Dealer

Tobias was late. He'd gotten stuck in traffic on the freeway, and now he was going to be an hour late to his friend Theresa's party. Tobias hated to be late generally, but this time he was particularly put out because he knew that Theresa was making her extra-special double-fudge chocolate-chip cake especially for him. She knew Tobias was crazy about the cake, that it sent him into a delicious chocolate stupor every time. And now he was sure he would miss out on a piece. This may not seem like such a big deal to you, but Tobias really and truly did live for chocolate. If the Betty Ford Center had a treatment for chocolate addiction, he probably would have been committed against his will long ago.

Finally the traffic eased and Tobias gunned the motor. With a lead foot on the accelerator, he raced to Theresa's house, finally screeching to a stop in front. Grabbing the bottle of wine he'd brought, he bolted from his car and ran up to ring the doorbell. When Theresa finally answered it ("Well, hello stranger!"), Tobias gave her a quick cheek kiss and an apology, then barreled past her to see what was happening at the food table.

Stopping short, he saw that there were still three pieces of his chocolaty delight waiting. Whew! He took a deep breath and got in the little line of folks who were still getting food. But to his horror, by the time he got to the end of the table where his beloved cake was, he saw that there was only one piece left—and Theresa's friend Jody was just about to lay her hands on it.

"Uh, Jody—hi," Tobias smiled. "Umm . . . I don't want to be obnoxious, but I was wondering if you'd . . . well, if you'd let me have the last piece of that cake." Jody looked a little puzzled. "It's totally yours and everything, but I gotta tell you, it's my favorite cake ever, and I think I just may die if I can't get a piece of it. And look! I can give you the last of the sushi. There's none left, and I'll give it all to you. Whaddya say?"

Jody was a bit taken aback. After all, she'd really wanted to try the cake. But she also loved sushi, and there really hadn't been enough for everyone. And besides, Tobias seemed really desperate to get his hands on the cake. She decided to compromise. "Okay Tobias, that's a pretty good offer. I'll take your sushi and give you the cake—but I do want one bite."

Hallelujah! Tobias pushed the sushi onto Jody's plate and was rewarded with a hunk of his dream cake—minus, of course, one bite. Well, he was pretty sure he could live with that.

We all find ourselves negotiating with other people all the time, even in the most superficial social situations. There's bound to be something that someone else has that you find yourself wanting. So how can you negotiate for it without pushing too hard? Check out these tips:

- **Find something the other person wants.** Is there anything you can offer that would compensate for what you're asking them to give up? This could be sushi, a ride home, or the seat next to someone they find attractive. Lots of times, people agree to negotiate just to maintain goodwill.

- **Keep your cool.** You don't want to give the impression that the thing you want is more important than the person you're negotiating with. Try to maintain a cool exterior and stay courteous.

- **Know when to give up.** Remember, no piece of cake is important enough to make an ass of yourself over. Try to remember that there will be a next time, and don't spend all of your social goodwill on this one particular thing.

# Loose Lips

Everyone indulges in a bit of gossip on occasion. When done wisely, swapping stories can build your intimacy with others and keep you in the know. But there are plenty of pitfalls that can turn harmless chatting into something awkward or downright hurtful.

Austin was a bit fast and loose when it came to gossiping. He loved to hear a good story, even about people he'd never met. His favorites were romantic intrigues and work gossip, and he enjoyed hearing these tales as much as sharing them.

One day he went to lunch by himself at a restaurant near his company's office in the financial district. He'd been having a tough time at work, and he wasn't feeling up to his usual company and chatter. He'd really blown it on his last two reports, and he knew this was going to reflect poorly on him during his upcoming employee evaluation. As he was drowning his sorrows in a double order of french fries, he overheard someone near him saying his name. He pricked up his ears just in time to piece together what the woman's voice was saying. "Yeah, that idiot Austin on the tenth floor completely messed up the year-end reports, and now I've got to fix them. You'd think they could learn to hire someone who knows what they're doing. But I hear he may be fired, because this is the second time he's blown it. I say good riddance."

He turned his head slightly and recognized the woman as someone he'd ridden in the elevator with on many a morning. They'd never actually met, but he knew she worked for his company. And how many Austins could have offices on the tenth floor in this town? His heart sank after getting that harsh dose of his own medicine, and he got up and returned to his office, wondering how long he'd still have an office.

You never know who might be listening when you're gossiping. Here are a few ways to try to minimize the damage you do to others:

- Try not to gossip in public. Restaurants are the worst. Sure, you can look around to see if the person in question happens to be sitting next to you. But you never know if their friend or acquaintance—someone you've never met—is sitting near you. It's not impossible that someone they know will put two and two together, figure out who you're dishing about, and tell that person you've been bad-mouthing them around town. Unless you're prepared to deal with the consequences, you may want to wait for the privacy of your home, or at least until you're in the car or taking a walk.

- If you leave a phone message for someone, don't gossip about them after you hang up unless you're completely sure that the call has been disconnected and there's a dial tone. Otherwise, you could be leaving more of a message than you bargained for, and that doesn't make for happy campers.

- Don't make a habit of mean or nasty gossip, and never make things up. If people know that you're talking trash about everyone all of the time, they're going to rightly assume that you're probably talking about them, too. It's not going to earn you a place in their heart, and it just may mean that they feel comfortable spreading what you say all over town.

Choose wisely. Don't dish about your close friend with someone you just met at a party. Don't complain about your boss to strangers. Assume that whatever you're saying is going to get back to the person, and you'll be less likely to sink your own ship with your loose lips.

# Think It Over

Do you find that you agree to requests in the moment, without giving yourself a chance to think things over? Are you the kind of person who can't say no? Do you have nightmares that your Palm Pilot is chasing you? If this sounds like you, you may need to set up a mandatory waiting period.

Marissa did just that, and it has revolutionized her life. She works as a PR person, and one of the perks of her job is that she meets interesting people all day long. At the end of countless meetings, her clients and colleagues ask her if she'd like to do lunch sometime *outside* of work. While Marissa knew that having to balance all of these great people was simply an embarrassment of riches, and she didn't want to complain, she also knew that between keeping up with her hectic work schedule and hanging out with all of her new and old friends, she was wearing herself to the bone. But how could she say no to all of these nice people without looking like she was trying to avoid them?

Before, she felt like she had to give someone an answer to their request right away—and her answer was almost always yes. Now she's instituted a waiting period to all requests, mainly because she knows that if she answers right away, she'll cave to the pressure. It may feel awkward at first, but you have the right in every conversation to get back to someone. If they're asking for a favor, you can always claim some time to mull over what you want to say. Especially if you have a hard time saying no (or, for that matter, saying yes), you may want to follow Marissa's lead and institute a twenty-four-hour waiting period before responding to any requests.

Here are sample answers when you need time to think it over:

- "Thanks for the offer. Let me check my calendar and get back to you."

- "I've been really busy lately. Let me make sure I have time before I say yes."

If someone presses you to make an instant decision, try these approaches:

- "Do you need an answer right now? Or is it okay for me to get back to you?"

- "If you need to know right now, I'm afraid my answer will have to be no."

And here's a nice way of saying no, should you decide to:

- "Thanks for the lovely offer. I'm swamped right now with work, but I look forward to chatting with you at the next big event."

Don't be afraid to resort to e-mail or voice mail at first, as you're working on your "no" skills.

# Flip Tip

Asking potential new friends to hang out can be almost as hard as asking that special someone out on a date. What if they don't like you and they say no? It can seem just as crushing as finding yourself at the bottom of Niagara Falls. So how do you take that risk?

When you make requests of others, give them the space to think over their decision. For example, instead of being a big bully and demanding an instant answer, it's always nicer to say something like, "I'd love to have lunch with you, if your schedule isn't too hectic. Give me a call if you get a chance." This lets people off the hook. They'll contact you if they have the time and the inclination, and if they don't have one or the other, you haven't forced them to say that to you in that very moment. If they do say no, there's no harm in convincing yourself that it's their time shortage that stifled your burgeoning friendship.

# Don't Try So Hard

There is no such thing as perfection, especially when it comes to human interaction. You may realize this while you're still straining to find the "perfect" thing to say. Well, guess what? Ain't no such thing, and the more you push to find it, the less likely it is that it'll pop out of your mouth.

Tina felt like she was moving underwater as she approached Glenn. She'd had a big crush on him for the past three months, and they'd struck up an acquaintance, but she still felt terrified every time she tried to approach him. Because she wasn't used to flirting, she was worried about sticking her foot in her mouth. Also, Tina had studied art history in school, and Glenn taught the subject at the local university. She was dying to talk to him about German Expressionism, both to hear what he had to say and also to impress the pants off him. But she was usually too uptight thinking about what she wanted to say to listen for a natural opening. She'd just rehearse her words over and over in her head, missing out on the conversation—and any real connection with Glenn.

This time would be different! She'd *make* it work. Sweating profusely, Tina broke into the little group Glenn was talking with. They were discussing a collection of drawings at the newest gallery in town. Feeling like her head was swathed in thick cotton, Tina struggled to find a place where she could insert her question about Expressionism and impress Glenn with her knowledge. After standing there for ten minutes, she couldn't stand it anymore. Right in the middle of the discussion about the new gallery owner's fashion sense, Tina blurted out "And how 'bout those German Expressionists, huh?" As the silence fell around her, Tina realized that maybe she was trying a little too hard.

We all want to say just the right thing to impress others and make ourselves look good. But when we're pushing for perfection, we're probably not participating in the give-and-take of good conversation. We're also not enjoying ourselves very much, and after all, isn't having fun the most important part of social interaction? If you're working overtime to be perfect in a conversation, what's the point?

Good conversations are about exchange—of ideas, attention, and energy. When we knock ourselves out trying to say just the perfect thing or make ourselves look good, we're not relaxing enough to let the exchange take place. This is sure to make for a spotty conversation and may even lead to outright embarrassment—as Tina found out.

The main way to be attractive and engaging in any social interaction is to relax and enjoy it. When you have to work hard at it, the strain shows. You'll find that people are much more likely to want to engage with you if you're actually having a good time and are relaxed enough to appreciate the give-and-take. No matter how clever or perfect your conversation, if you're trying too hard, those around you will pick up on it and will be unable to relax around you. On top of that, you probably won't have much fun.

So the next time you find yourself worrying about saying the right thing, stop a moment. Take a deep breath, smile, and really listen to what your conversational partner is saying. Respond from the heart, without thoughts of impressing anyone. The more you can naturally enjoy spending this time with those around you, the more you will shine. Pushing it will only dull your glow.

# Some Other New Harbinger Titles

*Eating Mindfully*, Item 3503 $13.95

*Sex Talk*, Item 2868 $12.95

*Everyday Adventures for the Soul*, Item 2981 $11.95

*A Woman's Addiction Workbook*, Item 2973 $18.95

*The Daughter-In-Law's Survival Guide*, Item 2817 $12.95

*PMDD*, Item 2833 $13.95

*The Vulvodynia Survival Guide*, Item 2914 $15.95

*Love Tune-Ups*, Item 2744 $10.95

*The Deepest Blue*, Item 2531 $13.95

*The 50 Best Ways to Simplify Your Life,* Item 2558 $11.95

*Brave New You*, Item 2590 $13.95

*Loving Your Teenage Daughter,* Item 2620 $14.95

*The Hidden Feelings of Motherhood*, Item 2485 $14.95

*The Woman's Book of Sleep,* Item 2493 $14.95

*Pregnancy Stories*, Item 2361 $14.95

*The Women's Guide to Total Self-Esteem*, Item 2418 $13.95

*Thinking Pregnant*, Item 2302 $13.95

*The Conscious Bride*, Item 2132 $12.95

*Juicy Tomatoes*, Item 2175 $13.95

*Facing 30*, Item 1500 $12.95

*The Money Mystique*, Item 2221 $13.95

Call **toll free, 1-800-748-6273,** or log on to our online bookstore at **www.newharbinger.com** to order. Have your Visa or Mastercard number ready. Or send a check for the titles you want to New Harbinger Publications, Inc., 5674 Shattuck Ave., Oakland, CA 94609. Include $4.50 for the first book and 75¢ for each additional book, to cover shipping and handling. (California residents please include appropriate sales tax.) Allow two to five weeks for delivery.

*Prices subject to change without notice.*